ONE
TATTERED
ANGEL

A TRUE STORY

D0359335

ONE TATTERED ANGEL

A TRUE STORY

BLAINE M. YORGASON

Gentle Breeze
PUBLICATIONS

Copyright © 1995 by Blaine M. Yorgason

All rights reserved. No part of this book may be reproduced in any form or by any means without permission in writing from the publisher, Gentle Breeze Publications, P.O. Box 1311, Draper, Utah, 84020. While the following account is true, certain names have been changed, and most of the dialogue has been reconstructed fictionally.

Artwork and cover design by Douglass Cole, Cairo Design Group.
Design and typesetting by Jane Clayson.

Portions of four chapters of this book were adapted from Blaine M. Yorgason's short story "The Warm Spirit."

Library of Congress Catalog Card Number: 95-71894

ISBN 1-57636-000-8

Printed in the United States of America

10 9 8 7 6 5 4 3 2

For Charity and my beloved Kath,
two of Heaven's daughters.
For all the Christ-like men and women
who have given Charity and us their love
through service.

And for all tattered angels everywhere.

Contents

	Charity	vii
	Introduction	1
1	A Suffering Little Child	3
2	A Dream of Warning	13
3	Foster Children	22
4	My Dream	25
5	Our Angel Finally Comes	27
6	Heaven Reveals a Name	36
7	We Make a Commitment	42
8	A Difficult Decision	45
9	The Birth Family Decides	47
10	The Worst Day of Kathy's Life	49
11	An Inspired Lullaby	53
12	The First Surgery	56
13	A Personality Becomes Evident	62
14	We Hear from the Birth Family	66
15	A Second Surgery	68
16	A Major Miracle	72
17	A Letter from Kathy	76
18	An Interesting Question	82
19	To Discomfort an Angel	86
20	My Own Personal Struggles	90
21	Praying for Death	93
22	A Startling Discovery	101
23	A Christmas Outpouring	105
24	The Dishwasher	111
25	The Warm Spirit	115
	The Rest of the Story	127
	Illustration	131

Charity

A little girl lay down in
bed. sick. and Red.
She lay so still, very ill, and
every day she takes
a pill.

She can not hear, she
can not see, her life is
difficult, to you and me.

No one knows how long
she'll stay but
she is very fray.

The great lord has
reasons for many things
but some don't make
sense to you and me.

But if there
comes a day she dies
there will be a tear
in every one's eye, who
even got a glimpse of
little Charity.

By Barbara Snow

(Charity's Friend)

Introduction

I have thought about this book for a long time—seven years, to be exact. And for most of that time I never expected to write the whole thing. It seemed too close, too personal. That I now feel good about doing so amazes me. It also amazes me that the idea of not writing it suddenly seems selfish and maybe even unkind.

Why? Because I have been forever blessed by each glorious moment of a tiny but incredible slice of eternity that God has given me—a slice of eternity that I can no longer, in good conscience, hold to myself.

Save for the fact that some names have been changed and some dialogue reconstructed, what follows is as true an account as I am able to make. Almost in fear and trembling, therefore, I present the following.

A Suffering Little Child

IT WAS Sunday, the morning of Christmas Eve. Over the hospital intercom the joyous sounds of Christmas were playing, though the music—the Christmas songs I had loved my entire life—could not break through. Instead, the noise in the room with the suffering babies drowned it out. Besides their crying and whimpering, between the two of them there was one IVAC intravenous infusion pump, one Kangaroo feeding-tube pump, two cardiac monitors, an Oximeter, an Esophageal Ph Probe monitor, and a Sleep Study machine, each beeping and humming and sounding what seemed like constant alarms to let the nurses at the Primary Children's Medical Center know when problems were developing.

This was not the new, gleaming white structure that now carries the Primary Children's Medical Center name but the old, red-brick hospital that once graced the upper reaches of the Avenues in Salt Lake

City. Fifty years before our time it must have seemed to the builders that it would always be spacious and modern. Yet by the twenty-fourth of December, 1989, as my wife Kathy and I sat with our suffering daughter in her crowded room on the fourth floor, the whole facility seemed woefully inadequate. There was no privacy—for us, nurses, doctors, or other patients; there was little room for more than one visitor per child; each room had at least two children as patients (and some had four or five); the hallways were always crowded with extra equipment as well as scurrying personnel, ambulatory patients, and curious visitors—well, I shouldn't go on. Nevertheless, I was feeling put out by the whole of it, not feeling in any part of me the Spirit of Christmas, and I guess it showed.

As the piercing alarm on our tiny adopted daughter's cardiac monitor sounded for maybe the tenth time in thirty minutes, indicating that a lead wire had pulled loose again, I rose to my feet in desperation.

"This place," I muttered to my wife, "is driving me crazy!"

She looked at me sympathetically. "I can tell you're upset, but I don't think it's the hospital's fault."

"Maybe—maybe not." I stared out the window as a Life-Flight helicopter lifted noisily on its way back to wherever it waited for critically ill little patients, another sign of the pain with which we were surrounded. Groaning inwardly, I turned back into the room. "No, it isn't the hospital. In fact, I feel very thankful for it and all these doctors and nurses. They're great, and I don't know what we'd ever do without them. It's just that . . . well, I can't take any more of this noise!"

"Don't you think it's because you're tired?" Kathy asked.

Well, she had a point. I hadn't slept all night, but had spent most of it at my daughter's side or downstairs in the library reading about her condition.

"Maybe," I admitted, "but I'm still getting out of here!"

"Where will you go?" Kathy asked, not trying to dissuade me. "It's Sunday morning."

"Yeah," I replied, "and Christmas Eve is tonight, so everything is closed. Maybe I'll just go wander the halls here in the hospital."

"The children in the other rooms are just as ill as our baby," she said gently, somehow understanding that it wasn't really the noise that was bothering me.

Slowly I nodded, while tears filled my eyes once again. "I . . . I just can't bear to see her suffer like this. All this pain just doesn't seem fair! If only there was something I could do!"

"Honey," my sweetheart chided softly, "we've done everything we can do, so we need to leave it to the Lord. Besides, you knew it would be like this when we agreed to bring her into our family. Don't you remember that we both promised, in prayer, that we wouldn't complain, no matter how bad things got?"

Slowly I nodded, knowing she was right and yet not for a moment wanting to admit it. Still—

It has become more and more clear to me through the years that I am one of those fortunate few who somehow managed, either through remarkable luck or the direct intervention of heaven, to entice a woman of vast spiritual superiority to spend her life with me. Where I believe in righteousness and steadfastness and courage, she embodies them. Where I give lip service to the principles of love and service, she reaches out to others in a way I cannot even begin to comprehend. And when I bring suffering upon myself or others because of my own foolishness, she is always there, lifting me, forgiving me, loving me.

Of course, she has her weaknesses too—one of them being a penchant for keeping under her wing a wandering troubadour of words whose dreams have most often seemed larger than his realities. Yet I love her dearly and am almost always willing to hear what she has to say.

So now, in the face of her uncompromising wisdom and undeviating determination to righteousness, I slowly sank back onto my chair. "I know I agreed, Kath, and I'm not complaining. At least I don't mean to be. I realize that God loves our little girl. But three surgeries in a month? Why doesn't He bless her with a little peace until she dies—either that or take her back right now. Since she's going to die anyway, why does she have to suffer so much?"

"I don't know, but I feel like she knows."

"Well, I hope so. If I could just talk to her, Kath; if I could just make certain that she understood, then maybe I could come to some understanding of my own. Only, I will never be able to talk to her—"

My wife just looked at me, the tears in her own eyes brimming over. Seeing her sorrow and suffering caused me, for a moment, to forget my own pain, and I gazed back at her, seeing past the hint of gray in her hair, the wrinkles appearing on her face, and the sagging signs of exhaustion both in and beneath her lovely eyes. And she *was* exhausted! Our daughter's incredibly bad health problems had taken a real toll on her, as they would on any loving mother who was giving twenty-four-hour-a-day care to a critically ill child.

Despite such transitory signs of aging and exhaustion, however, she still seemed to me so beautiful, so perfectly formed. Had it really been twenty-five years, I wondered, since I had first seen her exquisite face in the doorway of a store and known, instantly and with absolute certainty, that she and I were supposed to be one? It seemed such a short time since, frightened beyond belief, I had approached her with my hand outstretched, introduced myself, and asked her for a date.

With what some would consider great wisdom, she had turned me down. Knowing what I "knew" of our future, however, kept me going, and two weeks later we were engaged. Six weeks after that we were married. ("Don't you ever do this!" I have warned our children since. "After all, it took us two years just to get our names straight!") And for twenty-five years we had enjoyed together the happiness and vicissitudes of life. Mostly, though, we had been happy. Kathy had given birth to six wonderful children. One son was married and a daughter was preparing for marriage, and one would have thought (or maybe expected) that Kathy and I were ready for some years of peace and freedom.

Instead, here we were spending Christmas in the hospital with our tiny seventh child, suffering with her, aching for her, and trying to see some sort of hope for her through the haze of our sorrow and exhaustion. But how could there be hope with such a prognosis? How could there be a feeling of Christmas joy in such a climate of pain? I certainly didn't know, and I was far too tired to keep looking. All I wanted was to get out, to go some place far away and forget—

A bustling Santa Claus bounced suddenly into the room, wishing us a Merry Christmas and leaving a reindeer-crowned candy cane for each of the tiny, unresponsive patients. Moments later he was gone on his merry way, and I was feeling worse than ever.

"Look at that, Kath. She can't even enjoy Christmas! Why, oh why is God allowing this to be done to our baby?"

"I . . . I don't know," she replied softly. "I . . . I . . . wish I did. But I know Jesus loves her, and I know He loves all these other children here in the hospital. Understanding that, I am just as certain that these little ones and their families will all earn great blessings for what they are going through."

I nodded. "I . . . I believe that, too, Kath. It couldn't be any other way. I just . . . well, I'm tired of seeing this little angel of ours in so much pain—day after day, week after week, for sixteen months now! I don't know how much more I can bear to watch her suffer. If only she would smile again! I can't tell you how much I miss her smile and her cute little giggle.

"Now here it is Christmas, and while millions of children are happily anticipating tomorrow morning's toys, she's stuck here in the hospital without even the mental ability to understand what she's missing. What a lousy place to spend Christmas! What a lousy hand to be dealt in life!"

"You don't really feel like this," Kathy said softly as she put her hand on my arm. "I know you don't. I've heard you tell too many people how thankful you are that the Lord honored our family with a heavenly child."

I sighed and looked down at our little daughter, who appeared so physically perfect and yet had such great problems. One tube that ran into her nostril supplied food; it had been in place since the previous August, when she had somehow lost the ability to suck. Other tubes in her nose were for oxygen, helping her to breathe until the shock of her surgery was past. The wires on her chest and back monitored her heart and respiratory functions; these were the source of the constant-sounding alarm. Her orange, Betadine-swabbed, and completely shaved head, as well as the bandaged incisions there and on her stomach, spoke further of the new shunt that

9

had just been installed to drain excess fluid from her head to her abdominal cavity—a shunt that followed other similar devices that had all failed in their operation. For all we knew, this one would fail as well.

Our daughter lay still, but every moment or so she would writhe with pain as she whimpered and cried out for relief. The whole scene wrenched my heart more than I could imagine, and knowing that there was no real hope for her mortal future made the situation seem just that much worse.

I felt abandoned, without hope, and a bitterness was growing within me because it seemed as if this little girl I had grown to love more than life itself, as well as the woman who had always been my whole life, had also been abandoned. It was not fair for any of us, especially them! It was not—

Blinking back tears of despair, I finally left the room and made my way down the hall, looking neither to the right nor to the left and thus sparing myself further pain. The waiting room, I thought moments later as I sank into an empty couch, was at least a little more quiet, and the suffering patients were thankfully out of sight.

For once the TV was off, and other than the soft snoring of an elderly grandfather who had finally succumbed on a nearby couch after a long night's vigil, and the Christmas music that was playing softly over the intercom, the room was blissfully still.

Glancing around, I looked past the tattered magazines to an early edition of the Sunday paper that someone had left scattered on the floor. "Jerks!" I grumbled softly. "Where were they raised? In a barn?" For a moment I thought of gathering the paper and losing myself in it. Only somehow I didn't have the energy to even drag myself to it, let alone read. So I laid my head back, closed my eyes, and—and saw in my mind the terribly wounded form of my tiny daughter.

"No!" I breathed as I forced my eyes open again. "I don't want to see that. I can't bear to see it—"

Across the room stood a brightly decorated Christmas tree, a glowing angel perched on the uppermost needled spire. For a moment I studied her—I believe it was a her—noting her wings, the halo, the scepter in her hand. Everything about her looked rumpled, battered, crooked. The gold halo was down in front of her face, her scepter was bent, her wings were crooked, and I could see a tear in her dress—

"Looks like a kid decided to play with her," I muttered grimly, my heart filled with disgust. "Or maybe a dozen kids, the way she looks. Good grief! With all the money they take in, you'd think the hospital could afford some decent Christmas ornaments! Cheapskates!"

Over the intercom someone was singing, *"Hark, the herald angels sing, glory to the newborn King."* Tearing my eyes from the tattered angel, I found myself thinking again of my little girl, her tiny body savaged by the medical procedures she had been forced to endure.

"Oh, man!" I thought as I closed my eyes against this vision. "How did I ever let myself get into such a mess? How had I let Kathy get into it? How had it begun, this excruciating and protracted journey with a little girl who could not possibly survive? Haltingly then my mind started back, probing, remembering—

A Dream of Warning

"BLAINE, are you awake?"

"Mmmph," I replied groggily. "I . . . am now."

"I just had the most wonderful dream! Wake up so I can tell you about it."

It was the fall of 1983, so early the light was only barely showing outside our window, and I was not in a joyful mood. In fact, I remember dampening Kathy's excitement a little by telling her that anything dreamed that early in the morning sounded more like a nightmare than a dream. She remained convinced, however, that the Lord had revealed some important information to her, and she wanted me to know of it.

"All right," I finally grumbled, leaning on my elbow and trying to focus my eyes in the early morning gloom. "Tell me your nightmare."

"It was a wonderful dream," she began, staring up at the ceiling with a soft smile on her face. "I dreamed we were going to have another baby—a little girl."

"Yep. Sounds like a nightmare, all right."

"Blaine!"

Recovering from her light blow, I grinned. "I'm sorry, hon. I'll be serious."

"Yeah, right you will."

"I mean it. I'll try. Now, let's hear about this little girl we're supposed to have that we both know you can't have."

I was only partly teasing, for it was true that Kathy could never give birth to another child. A ruptured uterus during labor and an emergency hysterectomy following the birth of our sixth child, Michelle, had rendered her physically incapable. Yet here she was, all excited about another baby. "Baby hungry" was a term she often used when holding other women's children, and that was obviously her problem now. About all I could do, therefore, was smile and listen and wait for her "hunger" to pass.

"She was a newly born baby, Blaine, very tiny and so cute. I had her in an infant seat, but she had on no clothing but a diaper and a thin receiving blanket, and I was worried about her getting cold. Though she looked perfectly normal and healthy, I was trying desperately to get her to a hospital for care. Only for some reason I kept falling down, getting the baby all wet and cold. Yet she never cried or complained. She just smiled and loved me.

"Another thing was that people kept stopping me to see her and tell me how beautiful she was. And she was beautiful, Blaine! She had dark hair, dark eyes, a beautiful complexion, and an incredible smile—she was so perfect, and I was so proud of her. But I had to get her to that hospital—"

"Why?" I asked, trying not to sound too interested.

"I don't know. She looked perfect, but she seemed to have a health problem I couldn't see."

"Sounds like a strange dream, Kath. Like I said, a nightmare, something we don't want anything to do with."

"You didn't feel that way in the dream."

"There's more?" I groaned, realizing she hadn't yet mentioned any part I had played in her dream.

Kathy smiled at my hammed-up distress. "A little. When I finally got to the hospital, you were there waiting for me. You took our little girl from me, hon, and told me that everything was going to be just fine. You absolutely loved her! I have never seen such a look of pure happiness on your face as when you held her."

"I doubt that," I said, dropping back onto the bed. "Why?"

"Because I hate hospitals! I don't like sickness or being around sick people. You can bet I wouldn't be happy there."

"It wasn't the hospital that made you happy, silly. It was our little daughter. You loved her more than I can say, and that love glowed all over you just like a light."

"I doubt that, too," I declared, feeling a little less jovial. "Think about it, Kath. For us to get a little girl means we would have to adopt her. Occasionally I've thought about adoption, and to tell you the truth, I don't think I could love someone else's child the way I love my own."

"Sure you could."

"No I couldn't," I declared, warming to the subject. "Other peoples' kids bother me, Kath. They really do! I think the vast majority of them are obnoxious and spoiled, and I don't even like being around them. Not, at least, until they're teenagers.

"But there's another problem, a much larger one. We've already had our family. They're all growing up now, finally giving us the freedom to go off by ourselves, without worry, to enjoy life. Besides, my books are doing well, very well. Doubleday has accepted *Massacre at Salt Creek* for publication, and the stage play based on *Charlie's Monument* is touring the western United States. The movie based on *The Windwalker* has done great, too, and now that it has won those awards we might even see more of my books made into movies. Whether that happens or not, I believe we need to take advantage of every opportunity we have to keep going."

I did, too. I had ended my high school teaching career six years before and had moved my family to Utah, a state absolutely overflowing with gorgeous mountains and deserts. Here, I felt, I could not only pursue my studies of western American history, but, inspired by the scenic grandeur around me, could begin writing the historical novels that were busily agitating my mind. During our six years in Utah my writing career had gone better than I had hoped, much better, and I could see no reason it shouldn't continue.

"We have a lot of traveling and research to do, Kath," I concluded. "A lot of places to see and people to meet, and a baby such as you dreamed of would really mess things up."

"Sounds kind of selfish, don't you think?"

"No, I don't. We've earned the blessings, and now I believe it's time to enjoy them!"

What I was really saying, of course, was that I was too busy being "rich and famous," as my kids put it, to mess with other people's problem children. Which, when it comes to it, *was* selfish. And extremely unrighteous, too. At the time, however, it didn't feel that way at all.

"Blaine," Kathy continued, changing the subject just a little, "I think I should begin to look for her."

"And I don't," I said, feeling more and more irritated. "I'm telling you, Kath, that would ruin our lifestyle, and I'm not about to let that happen!"

For a moment or two my wife was silent. The room was somewhat lighter, and the birds in our London Plane trees outside the window were warming to their dawn chorus. Everything had seemed so peaceful, so promising. But now this—

"I can see," Kathy suddenly said, her voice quiet, "that Heavenly Father is going to have to humble you."

Kathy has always called God "Heavenly Father," which she says makes Him seem more personal.

"What?" I groused. "Humble me? I already am humble! I just—"

"I saw our little girl," Kathy said, stopping me in midsentence. "I know it, and I know we're supposed to have her. But she won't come as long as you feel this way. So starting this morning, I think we should pray that she will come. I'm going to, anyway. And I'm also going to pray that you will be humbled enough to accept her and love her—"

I probably should have been terrified by Kathy's pronouncement, for long experience has taught me that she usually gets what she prays for. Unfortunately I paid no attention to her but went on my merry way, blissfully ignoring the faith she was exercising in my behalf. After all, it seemed I could do no wrong in my writing affairs, and my opinions were highly valued and sought after by others. Surely, I thought, I would be right about this dream baby as well.

As it turned out, however, the Lord not only heard Kathy's prayers but sided with her in her opinion of my humility—or lack thereof. In confirmation He provided a second witness. Shortly after Kathy's dream, my mother called to tell us that she had also had a dream, wherein she had seen Kathy presenting me with a new little baby. "But," she warned direly, "you will not get this child unless your family is better prepared for her."

"Thanks, Mom," I said, stifling a yawn. "We're trying to teach them, but you know how kids are these days—"

From the perspective of 20/20 hindsight, I truly wish I had paid attention to these two women. That I didn't was apparently a sign to God that my humility muscles had atrophied into nonexistence. So—

Life rather quickly began getting harder. Besides the normal horrors that came with trying to help guide six children through their teenage angst, I began making some very foolish business decisions. I went deeply into debt on a speculative venture, mortgaging to the hilt every asset I had, and hoping against hope that it would all work out. It didn't. Within two years from Kathy's dream and the commencement of her prayers, through no fault of anyone but myself, I had lost everything in this world except my family and my pride. And six months later, still being battered by the world, my family was reeling, and even my pride was starting to waver.

"Are you still praying for me to be humbled?" I moaned at my wife one night near the end of 1985.

"Every day." She smiled sweetly.

"Well, knock it off, will you? If I get any more humble, it's going to kill me!"

"Or save you. Are you ready for our little girl yet?"

"Kath—"

"I mean it, Blaine. She's a special baby, and the Lord will not send her to our home until we are spiritually ready for her." Abruptly her look softened. "But don't feel so bad, hon. It isn't just you that is being humbled. The Lord is working his miracle on all of us, the kids and me included. More and more I have the feeling that our little girl is truly an angel from heaven, and the Lord wants us all to be ready when she comes."

"You really think we're changing?"

"Well, we're certainly not perfect, if that's what you mean." Kathy smiled again. "But I do see some promising signs."

"Such as?"

"Such as not so much fighting between the kids."

"Or us?"

"That, too. Our prayers feel more meaningful. I know mine are, and I think yours have changed, too. Our family Bible study is more regular, the kids' grades in school are going up, and our TV consumption is dropping. I believe these are all positive changes."

As I thought about it, I had to agree. Lately, because I had literally been forced to my knees, I had found myself constantly repenting before the Lord of both big and little things I seemed so easily to slip into. More significantly, I was actually starting to get clearer answers to my own prayers. Those changes were amazing to me, for I had been trying to change for years and had never pulled it off.

My writing was also changing, growing more sober, more difficult, maybe even more honest. No longer did my words skip willy-nilly like flat, dead stones flung across the unexplored waters of my life. Rather, harsh circumstances were forcing me to face myself more squarely, seeking, pondering, probing, asking, praying, feeling, acknowledging not only embarrassing weaknesses but occasional wonderful attributes that I had never dared hope might exist.

Such changes in myself were surprising. But what really amazed me were my children. Three or four times in the past few months I hadn't been able to scrape enough money together to pay the utilities or car payment. Each time my older kids had voluntarily chipped in entire paychecks from their part-time jobs and paid the bills for me (is that humbling enough?). And in the most destitute yet memorable Christmas of my life, I had tearfully watched my family open sweet and thoughtful gifts from an unknown Santa Claus who turned out (why was I surprised?) to be my own children—the teenagers I had thought a year or two before were going to heck in a handbasket.

Well, at least one of us had been—

3

Foster Children

"See? I knew you would love them!"

"How could anybody love anything this small," I grumbled while cradling the tiny infant in my arms. Of course I was teasing, for I was absolutely amazed at how easy it was to cuddle this little boy whom I'd never even heard of until the day before.

"I don't know why," Kathy continued as she mixed formula and warmed the baby's bottle, "but I couldn't get rid of the feeling that we needed to become foster parents."

"I sort of thought they'd come a little bigger."

"I told you I signed up for the newborns. I feel like we have to do this, Blaine, before we can obtain the little girl the Lord has promised us."

As I watched my wife, filled with wonder at her tenacity, I realized she might very well be right. But even if she wasn't, I was absolutely enjoying these little children who were coming to stay with us a week or so before going on to their real adoptive homes.

Those were wonderful times as "our" foster children passed one after another through our home. As I held and cuddled and helped nurture those tiny little people, each of whom came to us with different problems and different skin colors, I came to see how wrong I had been. I absolutely loved those children, every single one of them! I loved them as much as I loved my own, and it made not a particle of difference that other men had been their fathers—other women their mothers. Each of them was a choice soul, and I felt honored to be allowed to meet and get to know them in the two or three weeks each stayed with us.

Our own children felt the same way, excitedly taking turns giving each new child a temporary name. An Oriental girl we named Stephanie after a neighbor one of our sons had a crush on, and an Indian boy we named Justin—Chief Justin, we called him, of the Supreme Court. He was a bellower, another reason we called him that, and just as cute as a button. Our children loved them all, held them, fed and even changed them, sometimes got up at night with them when we were too tired, and wept with my wife and me each time one of them left our home to begin his or her new life elsewhere. Yet the weeping was joyful, too, for we all knew "our" babies were on to bigger and better things with a family all their own.

But while we watched other families being blessed, our little girl failed to appear. Social Services, in approving us for foster care, had stated emphatically that foster families were never considered for adoption. We had agreed to that and so never looked for our little girl to be among our foster babies. We simply waited while we cared for those sweet children who were going to bless the lives of others, convinced that our own divinely appointed daughter was coming but leaving her manner of arrival, as well as the timing of it, up to the Lord.

And then I had a dream.

4

My Dream

"KATH," I said as early one morning as I could force open my eyes, "I think I saw her."

"Who?"

I gave an exaggerated sigh. "Who? Who are you always talking about? I think I saw our little girl."

Kathy looked at me incredulously. "Really?"

"Well, it was my turn, you know. I mean, if the Lord is going to give everybody else in this family dreams—"

Kathy smiled patiently. "So what did you see?"

"I saw Nate holding a tiny baby girl on the couch in the family room. I think it means she'll be coming sometime after he gets home from Arizona next spring. Let's see . . . That will be May of 1988. So expect your little baby sometime after that."

"Like a month?" Kathy's smile turned mischievous. "Or a year? Or maybe a decade? Are you really even sure it was her?"

And because I wasn't, and because I can hardly bear wives who persecute their perfectly wonderful husbands, my only defense was to grab my wife's ribs and start tickling.

Amazingly, it turned out that I was right.

5

Our Angel Finally Comes

"Hello. Is Kathy at home?"

"She certainly is," I replied to the woman on the phone. "Just a moment, and I'll call her."

I did so and then idly balanced the receiver on my shoulder while I waited for my wife to pick up the phone in the kitchen. It was Wednesday, August 31, 1988. Nate had been home three months and had already moved into an apartment with some friends. I was at my easel, painting an illustration that was to be used as the cover for one of my books.

The woman's voice had sounded familiar, sort of like Sharon, the woman who had overseen our efforts as a foster family. But it had been nearly a year since our last baby, and we had assumed that the "foster family" period of our lives had concluded. Which was a good thing, I thought a little grimly, for our financial "humbling" had continued, bringing with it the loss of our home. Now we were in the middle of packing and looking around for a home to rent—a mission that was feeling more and more impossible. Not a good time, I thought, to be taking in any new foster babies.

Kathy said hello, and I was not surprised to hear the woman identify herself as Sharon. Normally I would have hung up at that point, but for some reason I felt like eavesdropping and left the phone on my shoulder.

"Kathy," Sharon asked, "are you available to take another foster baby?"

"Of course," Kathy replied without hesitation. "When?"

"Probably tomorrow. I'll call you."

"Sounds wonderful. Is it a boy or a girl?"

"She's a darling little girl. Uh . . . you might have her a little longer than the usual week or so. Will that be a problem?"

"I don't think so. Why? Is something the matter?"

"Well, she has some health problems. She's hydrocephalic, and she was born without a cortex. It may take us a while to find an adoptive family. If we don't find one, we'll probably have to place her in an institution."

Hydrocephalic and no cortex, I thought as I listened in. It sounded serious, though truthfully I had no clue what those things meant.

"Well, don't worry," I suddenly realized my wife was saying. "If you can't find anybody to adopt her, we will!"

"What!" my mind screamed into the silence that hung between Kathy and Sharon, completely spacing out Kathy's dream of a little girl who was being rushed to a hospital. What was she thinking? Didn't we have enough problems already? Did we have to go around volunteering to shoulder others? She was crazy! And besides that, she—

"You would do that?" Sharon was asking, her voice incredulous.

"Of course we would. She deserves a family like anyone else, doesn't she?"

My mind spinning with the magnitude of what Kathy had just offered to do, I listened as Sharon thanked her and promised to call the next day. Carefully then I hung up and made a beeline march for the stairs. Moments later Kathy and I were seated across from each other in the kitchen.

"Do you have any idea . . . " I started to demand, and then I noticed her tears. "Kath, what is it?"

"I . . . I don't know," she stammered, her voice little more than a whisper. "I had the . . . strangest feeling, when Sharon was talking to me. Blaine, I . . . think this little girl is *our baby*."

"What?" For the first time in months those memories of her dream, as well as my own, came back to me. "Our baby?"

"Uh-huh. Remember how I was hurrying her to a hospital?"

"Well, sure, but—"

"Blaine, I think this is her! That's why I said what I did about taking her. I know foster parents aren't supposed to adopt or even to request it. But the feeling that she is to be ours was so strong I just couldn't help it!"

For a moment I was silent, digesting Kathy's news. "Do you know what Sharon was talking about—the things that are wrong with the baby?"

Kathy shook her head. "Not exactly. I'm pretty sure hydrocephalus is water on the brain. I remember reading that somewhere. And I think the cortex is a membrane, though I'm not certain where it is. But it won't matter, not any more than the fact that we're foster parents. If this little girl is the baby we've seen in our dreams, then Heavenly Father is going to see that we have her, no matter what."

Seeing the tearful look of determination on my wife's face was more than I could withstand. "You know," I said as I drew her to me, "you're really something, you know that? If this *is* our little girl, she'll be coming because she wants to be near you. And I don't blame her."

The day passed fairly normally, and I thought about the coming baby only when I wasn't dealing with the school registration problems Michelle was experiencing or a housing possibility for our family that was suddenly falling through.

"Kids," Kathy declared that night at supper, "we're getting a new baby tomorrow."

"Serious?" fifteen-year-old Dan asked. It was interesting to see how much he loved babies. It was a wonderful quality I would never have known about had we not entered the foster parent program. "Boy or girl?"

"She's a little girl," Kathy replied.

"*Yes!*" thirteen-year-old Michelle shouted as she

clenched her fist triumphantly. "Finally, after all those goofy boys!"

"Boys aren't goofy!" Dan declared in a heat. I should say that Dan and Michelle had been arguing since even before Michelle had learned how to talk. We had tried every way we knew to stop them. I had even turned them over to God, like Kathy had done with me. Only, apparently, they had been even harder cases than I had been, for God had not accomplished a thing with them. Neither had we.

"Oh, yeah?" This was Michelle again, defiant as ever. "You try changing boys' diapers and see how you like getting squirted!"

Travis, eighteen and also a connoisseur of good arguments, smiled but amazingly did not enter into the conversation, which I considered fortunate. Travis, too, was affected by the babies. But he didn't like the pain when they left, so he tried to avoid having as much contact with them. Which wasn't hard, considering the huge number of hours he was putting in at his job.

"We may need a little extra help with this one," Kathy continued. "She has what I think is water on the brain, and she's missing a membrane somewhere. Whatever, it's serious enough that Sharon might not find a family right away. May we count on your help?"

Soberly the kids nodded.

"Is this *our* baby?" Dan asked abruptly.

"I don't know, Danny. I suppose she might be. But whether she is or not, let's remember to pray for the baby's health and to ask Heavenly Father to see to it that she goes to the right family. Okay?"

Again the kids nodded soberly. And I was probably the most sober one of all.

The next day Kathy drove to the Social Services office and returned with the baby. I will never forget my first sight of her. At two days of age she was tiny, less than five pounds, and as I took her I remember thinking that I could easily have held her in one hand. She had lots of dark hair, her dark eyes were wide open, and so far as I could tell, everything about her was perfect. I even examined her tiny head for signs of swelling from too much fluid, though I could find none at all. Except for a slightly recessed forehead, she seemed perfect to me, absolutely beautiful, and I thought that if she wasn't ours, somebody was surely going to be blessed.

"Well, little one," I asked as I cradled her in my arms, "are you the baby girl we've been waiting for all these years?"

Her only answer was a little fussing and kicking, which served to get her hoisted away and into the anxious arms of Michelle. There a small bottle was plopped into her mouth, silencing her at least temporarily and giving Kathy and me a moment to talk.

"Now that you've seen her," I asked after we had made our way upstairs into my office, "what do you think?"

Kathy smiled. "I think she's our daughter, Blaine. I really do."

"Why?"

"I don't know. Just a feeling, I guess. Besides, she looks like her, though I don't remember her being this tiny."

"Maybe you saw her in your dream when she was a little older. Did you learn any more from Sharon?"

"Only that she wants to take her to Primary Children's Medical Center in Salt Lake City for some tests."

"What kind of tests?"

"I don't know."

"So, can we adopt her?"

"Well, Sharon says the agency is considering us. What they do is run a computer search through all the families in America that have been approved for adoption. If no one wants her, then they consider alternatives such as us."

Slowly I shook my head. "We'll never get her then," I said, feeling unaccountably sad. "She's so cute that thousands of families will want her!"

"Honey," Kathy said as she reached for my hand, "just have faith. If she is meant to be a part of our family, it will work out just fine."

Kathy was right and I knew it. Only the odds against it seemed so high that I didn't even dare hope. And I wanted to hope in the worst way. For suddenly, after having held her at most for five minutes, I wanted this little girl to be my daughter. It made no sense at all, but I did. I was head over heels in love with her. And that night, as we sent our petitions heavenward, mine was one of the most fervent pleas of all.

The next day we accidentally learned the nature of the baby's "missing membrane." One of our friends, a nurse at a hospital in a neighboring community, dropped by to visit with Kathy. When Kathy told her we had a new foster baby, she began waxing eloquent over a tiny baby that had been born at her hospital a couple of days before.

"She was so cute!" she exclaimed. "Even though she didn't have a brain, she was the most alert baby in the nursery, holding her head up and looking around just like she knew what she was doing. Everyone fell in love with her. If I could adopt her, I'd do it in a minute!"

The conversation drifted to other things, and as she was leaving, Kathy took our friend in to see "our" baby.

"Why," she exclaimed with surprise, "that's her! That's the baby girl I was telling you about—the one without a brain."

"She doesn't have a brain?" Kathy asked, astounded. "But how can she live?"

Margie smiled. "Well, she does have a brain stem. It runs the autonomic nervous system. All babies use it exclusively when they are first born, which is why this baby seems so normal. Later on, in six weeks or so, when she would normally begin to shift functions into the two hemispheres of her brain, this little girl will start having problems. It isn't likely that she will live long after that."

After the kids had all gone to bed, Kathy and I talked late into the night, thinking, wondering, probing each others' feelings. Suddenly this was a whole different situation than we had anticipated and dreamed of, and neither of us knew exactly what to do or how to feel. Health problems we thought we could deal with. But such a terrible and permanent disability seemed absolutely overwhelming, as did the possibility of so soon a death.

The next morning we lay in each other's arms, continuing to share our feelings about the tiny child in the bassinet across the room. Despite her massive problems, both of us felt that this was the child we had seen in our dreams, the special little girl the Lord had promised to send us and for whose reception we and the kids had been trying to prepare. With God's help, we were beginning to believe that we could take care of her.

Now if only the Lord would also tell the people at Social Services that we were the family—

Heaven Reveals a Name

"Look at this, everybody. This is amazing!" A couple of days had passed, and Kathy had been making a batch of cookies while the rest of us were finishing breakfast and getting ready for school, work, and so forth. Sharon had not yet arrived to take the baby to the hospital, which was that day's agenda, and she was lying quietly in a car seat on the counter, already fitting in as part of our family.

"What is it?" I asked, getting up to see what Kathy was so excited about.

"These cookies. This child's entire head is smaller than one of these cookies! I can't get over how tiny she is."

"She's little, all right," I said as I leaned over and kissed her forehead. "Little and cute!"

"What are we going to name her?" Dan was always concerned about names for our babies.

"Any ideas?"

Two or three names were tossed about, but somehow none of them felt right.

"I have a suggestion," Kathy said. "Since she's Heavenly Father's special child, why don't we have Dad pray and ask what God would want her to be named."

"Kath," I responded, feeling uneasy with such a burden, "I don't—"

"Yeah, Dad," Travis said as he piled the dishes in the sink. "You're the father here, so it should be your responsibility to at least find out if God cares what she's named."

"He'll care," Michelle interjected. "God always cares!"

Dan walked over and took the little girl's tiny hand in his fingers. "I don't really care what we name her," he said as he gazed tenderly at her, "just as long as it isn't one of those dumb names out of the Bible."

"Danny!"

"Well, knowing Dad," he replied defensively as he grabbed his books and headed for the door, "that's probably what he'll come up with. Jezebel or Hephzibah or something else just as stupid."

Ducking to avoid the slipper I had thrown at him, he grinned and was gone. A little later, after Sharon had come and taken the baby, I was alone on my knees in my bedroom, Dan's words ringing in my ears as I asked prayerfully about a name for the little girl I was positive would be our daughter.

For some time as I prayed, all sorts of thoughts raced through my mind, and I was finding it difficult to focus. Worries about the child's health, about how we would take care of her while we were moving, about how we would afford the medical expenses I knew would come with her—these worries and many more swirled around and around in my mind. Yet again and again I came back in prayer to the issue of her name, pleading to know if the Lord had a name He wanted us to call her.

It was only gradually that I realized a scripture was bouncing around in my head, a scripture from the New Testament. But thinking of Dan's admonition, I pushed the thought aside, only to find it there again moments later. Finally, with a sigh of resignation, I got up and walked to the nightstand, picked up the Bible, and for a change turned right to the verses I had been considering. Beginning at verse four of 1 Corinthians, I read: "Charity suffereth long, [and] is kind; charity envieth not; charity vaunteth not itself, is not puffed up, doth not behave itself unseemly, seeketh not her own, is not easily provoked, thinketh no evil; rejoiceth not in iniquity, but rejoiceth in the truth; beareth all things, believeth all things, hopeth all things, endureth all things. Charity never faileth."

Slowly I read the verses again, somehow knowing even as I read that these words perfectly described our little girl. More, I also felt certain that the Lord wanted her to be named Charity.

"Charity?" Kathy responded a little later when I showed her the scripture. "I like that name. It fits her. She certainly is a patient little thing. And if she doesn't have a brain, she'll never think evil thoughts or rejoice in iniquity."

"Or be puffed up with her own importance," I added, remembering too vividly my own past struggles. "But I had some interesting feelings while I was praying, Kath. I felt again that she is to be our daughter."

Kathy smiled.

"But more than that, the thought came to me that this is not a current decision, if that makes any sense. I'm not sure I understand this, but I believe that all of us, including Charity, agreed to be a family long before any of us was born. And so it is going to happen no matter how many families want her."

"Well, you know what I've been feeling—"

"It will happen. But Kath, I also had the feeling that Charity willingly accepted her birth defect, in part, at least, because it would help her come to us. In spite of that," and suddenly I found my eyes tearing up, "she is an incredibly righteous and powerful soul with a brilliant and active mind. It doesn't matter what handicaps having no physical brain will bring. I know she will always be aware of us and cognizant of what is transpiring around her. The Lord has not simply abandoned her here with no means of communicating with either Him or us. Through the power of the Holy Spirit I believe she will do both."

"Do you mean something like angels visiting her?"

I grinned. "Yeah, something like that. It'd be great having a bunch of angels hanging around here, wouldn't it?"

That evening when the family was gathered together, I read the scripture and told of my feeling about naming our little girl Charity.

"I don't like it," Michelle said bluntly. "Like Danny said, it's a Bible name."

"Well, at least it isn't a dumb one," Dan replied easily.

"I think it's dumb. And I think you ought to go back and pray again, Dad. I think Heavenly Father ought to give us a choice."

"Are you serious?" I asked.

"Yes," she replied, and I could tell that she was. "Go do it right now, before we go to bed. I want a choice."

Looking at my wife for help, I found none, only a smile and a slight shrug of her shoulders. So, with a sigh of resignation, I headed again for the bedroom, certain that no inspiration would come.

Apparently, however, God was as concerned about Michelle's feelings as He was about the little child's name, for almost instantly I felt to get my scriptures and read them again. I did so, finishing Paul's chapter I had started earlier, and as the Holy Spirit again bore witness I found myself chuckling, absolutely amazed at the Lord's sense of humor.

"Did you get an answer already?" Michelle asked, surprised at my rather sudden appearance.

"Yep!" I smiled. "And you were right. We have a choice—actually, of three names."

"Really?" Michelle was very excited.

Feeling good I sat back down. "Uh-huh."

"Well," Kathy asked, as interested as any of the kids, "what are they?"

Still smiling, I held up the Bible and looked at Michelle. "It says right here, Faith, Hope, or Charity. You decide, Sis."

"Faith or Hope?" Michelle rolled her eyes in disgust. "Those aren't choices! They're worse than Charity."

"Those are the three names God gave me."

"Well," she declared with an exaggerated sigh, "then I guess I have to pick Charity."

"So did the Apostle Paul," I told her. "In fact, he said Charity was the greatest of the three."

"Really?" she asked innocently, and we all laughed together. Suddenly she jumped to her feet. "I vote that we make Charity's middle name Afton, after Grandma Wagstaff. All in favor raise their hands."

We all did, knowing that our new little girl now had a name—Charity Afton. We just didn't know if it would ever become official.

We Make a Commitment

THE TESTS conducted at Primary Children's Medical Center confirmed what our friend Margie had told us—little Charity Afton had no brain. The medical term for her problem was hydranencephaly. In a letter dated 2 September 1988 and written to Sharon (but which we did not see until I was preparing this manuscript), Dr. Marion L. Walker, chairman of Pediatric Neurosurgery at PCMC, wrote:

> Her CT scan demonstrates severe brain loss in the supratentorial compartment. She has some occipital lobes bilaterally and normal appearing basal ganglia, thalamus, brainstem and posterior fossa. She essentially has no visible temporal, parietal or frontal brain. There is no indication in this CT scan to suggest increased intracranial pressure.

IMPRESSION: 1. Severe developmental anomaly. 2. Severe loss of brain substance bilaterally secondary to probable intra-uterine stroke.

This patient has very little potential for development beyond the infant stage. With almost complete loss of supratentorial brain, she has essentially no chance of developing beyond infant skills. Children with this much brain damage rarely survive childhood. Although some may live four to five years or possibly longer, it is unusual for these children to live beyond eighteen months.

As Sharon explained it to us the day after the tests and examination, the doctors had told her that Charity would be unable to enjoy any of her senses. She wouldn't be able to see, hear, feel, taste, or smell. She would know nothing of what was going on around her; would never have any control over any part of her body; would never experience or be able to express joy, happiness, and love; and would simply live her life in a vegetative state. She would also contract practically every disease and illness that came along, especially colds and flu, and would very likely die in the near future from pneumonia.

On the plus side (if these could be called pluses), the doctors had said Charity wouldn't grow very much or get very heavy, she would never feel any pain, her immune system would be pretty much non-existent, and she wouldn't have to endure this life for very long.

"Do these things matter to you?" Sharon asked us.

"No," Kathy replied firmly, "not at all. If she needs a home, we'll be happy to give it to her."

I gulped and nodded in agreement.

"Very well." Sharon smiled. "As soon as we know something, I'll let you know. By the way, she was so darling up there at the hospital. She didn't fuss at all but held her head up and just seemed to watch what was going on. She's really an amazing little girl."

"We know," I said as I took Kathy's hand. "We think she's an angel."

"Yes," Sharon replied as she moved out through our door. "I believe she is."

A Difficult Discussion

"IF CHARITY doesn't have a brain," Travis asked one night after he came home from work, "can she really be alive?"

His question stunned us. "Do you believe she isn't alive?" I asked.

"I didn't say that. In fact, I believe just the opposite. I think she's as alive as we are. But other people don't feel like that, including a guy at my work. He was being a real jerk about it."

"Did you tell him about Charity?"

"Yeah, but I guess maybe I shouldn't have. He thinks we should just let her starve to death. 'Sure,' I told him, 'Just murder her and then go have lunch.' He's a major pain."

"A kid in school said the same thing," Dan piped in. "I told him if she was breathing, that made her alive."

"So what happened?"

"Nothing. He knew I was right, so he shut up."

"Well," Travis said, looking exasperated and abruptly switching sides, "maybe you weren't. If they have no brain to think with, how can they be alive or have consciousness? If you don't let religion into the conversation, that's a darn good question."

"Yeah, but religion has to play a part too."

"Why?" Travis was enjoying this.

"Because we believe in it!" Dan growled.

"All right," I said, stepping in to referee, "just exactly how does religion answer the problem?"

Both boys looked at each other. "Because of their spirits," Dan replied first. "Paul says that God is the Father or Creator of our spirits, and like the bumper sticker says, God don't make no mistakes."

"What do you mean?" I pressed, surprised by Dan's knowledge of the Bible.

"He means," Travis interjected, "that despite the fact that they have no physical brains, and no matter how long they may live, from eighteen seconds to thirty years or more, babies like Charity are born with whole or perfect spirits. They have minds, they have consciousness, and despite their handicaps they are as much human beings as those who, say, happen to be born without arms or legs."

"Or even if they're born 'whole' like us," Dan added. "Isn't that right, Dad?"

I told them that I thought it was. As far as I was concerned, little Charity was as alive as any of us because her spirit was as whole as ours. And time, I felt, would prove us right.

The Birth Family Decides

"HONEY, Sharon called." Kathy sounded concerned. "The birth family wants to take Charity again."

"Why?" I asked as I turned from my computer, where I was drafting a new book. "What's going on?"

"I guess they're having a hard time letting go." She sat down at the end of my desk, and I noticed for the first time how drawn and tired she looked. Charity had not been sleeping well, and because we were a little older than we had been when our other children were tiny, we were both feeling the strain.

"I don't really blame them," she said as she rubbed and massaged her forehead. "If I was her mother or grandmother I couldn't bear letting Charity go. I think I'd rather die."

"I think it would be just as difficult for the men in her family," I argued.

"I'm sure you're right. Sharon says they're going to keep her at least through the weekend. She . . .

47

uh . . . she says some of the family are considering placing her in an institution."

"Seriously?"

"Well, that's what I've been told. Would you mind giving Charity a blessing before she goes?"

I looked at Kathy quizzically, thinking of the process of laying on of hands in prayer that we had been practicing in our family. "I guess so. What for?"

"So she can somehow communicate to the birth family that she is supposed to be our little girl."

Well, I am a believer in the Lord Jesus Christ and His infinite power, but that is not always the same as having faith in Him. Thankfully Kathy usually has enough faith for both of us. "Can I do that with a blessing?" I asked doubtfully.

Kathy smiled and rose to her feet. "*You* probably can't. But the Lord can do anything He wants. So if you'll pronounce the blessing, then the Lord can take over and bring her back to us. Sharon said she will be here in about thirty minutes, so when you're ready—"

I gave the blessing, and for the next three days we worried ourselves silly. Or at least I did. At last, however, Sharon returned with our little angel, bearing also the news that the birth family had finally felt peace about placing her for adoption.

As Sharon handed Charity to me, our three-week-old little girl burst into a radiant smile that did not go away for more than thirty minutes. As we basked in her smile's glow, we knew that Charity knew she was home!

10

The Worst Day of Kathy's Life

LATER that day, September 12, Social Services called and informed us that a computer search of the entire country had failed to turn up even one interested family. Therefore, if we were still interested, we could proceed with first qualifying for and then hopefully completing the adoption. Needless to say, our home rang that night with the joy of knowing our family would now be complete.

Unfortunately, the announcement also signaled the beginning of some real difficulties, both for Charity and for us. By the next day Charity was crying more than usual, and within a very few days she was crying almost continually. Examining her ourselves, we felt certain that her head was swelling, and this was confirmed on the 26th by our pediatrician, who for the first time thought he also heard a heart murmur.

Charity continued to cry and tremble until October 5, when in desperation we took her to the Primary

Children's Medical Center. There we met for the first time Dr. Walker, and he confirmed that her head was indeed enlarging. We appreciated his advice and enjoyed his tender approach, feeling relieved when he said he still hoped to avoid surgery to place a shunt but to come back in two weeks for further evaluation.

Although Charity seemed to do a little better in the next two weeks, our lives were truly coming apart. Especially this was affecting Kathy. Not only were we in the throes of our business failure, which was forcing us to move from our home, but also Kathy's physical health was starting to deteriorate. She'd had back problems off and on for years, but now they were coming back with alarming regularity, and there was no medical consensus on what was wrong. Worse, her father had grown desperately ill, and she was feeling torn between spending time with him and her mother and with our struggling little infant.

"Well, folks," Dr. Walker said after his follow-up examination on the 14th of October, "Charity's head is definitely enlarging. I would imagine she is becoming more irritable, too."

"She is," Kathy acknowledged. "She's been doing a lot of crying and a lot of trembling because of pain."

"Technically she isn't supposed to feel pain, you know."

"Well, we don't feel that Charity is a technicality. She's definitely in pain, and we know it."

Dr. Walker smiled. "I'm sure you're right. And she does respond to Tylenol, which would suggest the same conclusion. Changing the subject, I'd still rather avoid placing a shunt. There's a good chance this growth will stop and she will stabilize. Shall we try another two weeks and see her again?"

Somehow we all endured the next two weeks. On November 2 there was even more head growth, Charity's irritability and trembling had grown worse, and surgery looked very likely. However, Dr. Walker still wanted to wait one more week, hoping against hope that a shunt would not be necessary.

The wait was fine with us, though, for we knew we had to move that week. Fortunately we had located a home we could rent, so at least there was some peace about where we would be going. The following Monday we began to move. The health of both Charity and Kathy's father began to decline rapidly that same day, and on Tuesday the 8th of November I watched my dear wife experience what was no doubt the most difficult day of her life—at least until then.

"Blaine, something's going wrong with her. I mean really wrong!"

I was holding our screaming daughter at the moment, trying to comfort her, and finding no way to do so. "I know, Kath," I admitted. "I'm sure it's her head, but she isn't even responding to Tylenol any more. Besides, the bottle's empty—"

"We have more, don't we?"

"Somewhere." I looked around at the shambles in the home we were moving into. We had now slept there one night, so at least our beds were in place. But everything else was goodness-only-knew where. Our friend Max had been hauling loads of boxes in his pickup truck—a terribly needed gesture of friend-ship—but because I had been so involved with Charity I had no idea where he had been putting things. But, I thought, I could at least look around—

The telephone rang, our first call in the new home, and as Kathy answered it I watched her face drain of color.

"Dad's dying," she said as she replaced the receiver, a stricken look on her face. "I need to be with Mom!"

Moments later, trying desperately to make arrange-ments so she could go to her father's side, Kathy grabbed a bite of something to eat and broke off a major portion of her tooth, exposing nerves and leav-ing a jagged edge that quickly cut the side of her tongue to shreds. We were searching for some sort of pain-killer to deal with that and trying to locate our dentist, when the phone rang again and the school informed us that Michelle had run a sewing-machine needle completely through her finger and was at the hospital, needing a ride home.

Because I couldn't leave Charity, we found a neighbor boy, Ryan Wooden, who could go pick up Michelle. And Kathy managed to locate our dentist and have some temporary work done so she could go to her parents. Unfortunately, her father passed away before she could get there, which made her grief even harder to bear. And Charity cried all that night.

As I said, it truly was the worst day of my sweet-heart's life.

An Inspired Lullaby

ONLY A parent who has spent agonizing and sleepless nights with a sick child can know the feeling of helplessness it brings. There was a night, shortly after Dad's passing, that brought that home to me. Exhausted because of lack of sleep, Kathy and I were both in a dead stupor when, shortly after midnight, Charity again began to scream from pain.

Asking Kathy to remain in bed, I arose and took our anguished little girl downstairs, where I alternately prayed and wept, doing anything and everything I could think of to relieve her suffering—all to no avail.

It seemed so strange to me, this anguish of my daughter's. We had been told she would never feel pain, yet obviously she was suffering almost more than she could bear. She was also growing at a normal rate, although she had been expected to remain small. And on the rare occasions when she felt good, she smiled and responded exactly as our other children had done. Was it possible, I wondered, that the doctors had been wrong about her?

I didn't know, and of course at that moment I didn't really care. All I wanted was for her to be made free of pain. So as I sat and rocked, or stood and paced, I blessed her and prayed as fervently as I have ever prayed in my life, pleading that she be freed of the pain that seemed to be destroying her.

And then, sometime after three in the morning, I felt a great peace settle upon me, and as I wondered at it, the words and tune of a little lullaby began forming in my mind. Hesitantly I began to sing, and to my amazement Charity's crying stopped. With wide-open eyes she lay still, taking in every sound coming out of my mouth.

Though both the lyrics and tune were simple, Charity seemed to hang on every note, every word.

> *Oh Charity, pure Charity,*
> *Do you know who you are?*
> *Oh Charity, my Charity,*
> *An angel from afar.*
> *Our Father sent you to my home,*
> *For brief mortality.*
> *Oh Charity, smiling Charity,*
> *My Savior's gift of love to me.*

There were more verses than this, three more, describing my feelings about her pain, her becoming a part of our family, and her eternal destiny. Over and over I sang the verses, and as long as I was singing she was still, lying peacefully in my arms. Oh how I came to love her that night! I thought I had loved her before, but during those long hours we communed, spirit to spirit, and I truly felt of her sweet and gently perfect nature. She was indeed Christ's gift to me. I knew that with all my heart and soul, and suddenly I wanted more than I had ever wanted anything in my life to be worthy of her—and of Him—when I finally left this vale of sorrow and tears.

Sometime near daybreak Charity finally fell asleep, and a couple of hours later, after I had written down the lullaby and shared it with Kathy, she told me that a night or two earlier she, too, had been given a tender little song, one remarkably similar to mine, and it had had precisely the same affect. In listening, our little darling had somehow found peace and the courage to continue. And, in the face of her incredible courage, so did we.

The First Surgery

On November 17, when things had settled down a little at home, we took Charity back to PCMC, where Dr. Walker finally operated, performing a Right Ventriculoperitoneal Shunt Placement.

"Oh, Blaine," Kathy whispered in anguish when we saw her a couple of hours later, lying still but softly whimpering, "look at the poor little dear. Charity, Mommy's sorry—"

Charity did look awful. The right side of her head had been completely shaved of her beautiful hair, and her scalp was now covered with a red-orange substance that looked too much like blood to give me much peace.

"It's called Betadine," Dr. Walker said as he joined us. "It's a disinfectant. Charity tolerated the surgery quite well, but I thought you'd like to know exactly what we did."

"We would."

"All right. First we made an incision high on the side of her head, there under the bandage, and a burr hole was drilled through her skull. A ventricular catheter or shunt was inserted through the hole. The other end of the shunt was threaded beneath her skin down her neck and back, under her shoulder blade, around her side, and into her abdominal cavity. There a second incision was made to ensure correct placement. If you look carefully, you can see the tube there beneath her skin."

"That's a major surgery, isn't it?" I asked as I gazed at the raised skin covering where the tube lay.

"It is, especially for a child this tiny. We expect that the shunt will now drain the excess fluid from Charity's cranial cavity, thus relieving the pressure that has been causing her such distress."

"What if it doesn't work?" Kathy asked.

"Then we'll do it again." Dr. Walker smiled. "But don't worry. She'll most likely be just fine. I believe Charity's room will be on Four West. I'll probably see you there later today."

That afternoon, following post-operative recovery, Charity was transferred to Four West, a wing on the fourth floor, and there Kathy and I were first introduced to the sorrow, and the magic, of Primary Children's Medical Center.

But none of that was evident when we got there. Instead, Four West seemed very crowded, and that was about all I noticed. Charity was placed in a stainless-steel crib in a cubicle of a room in which were two other cribs, each with a tiny and very ill occupant. There were also three chairs, usually occupied by the three mothers, and considerable monitoring equipment. Finally, there was space in the center, but only a very little, for the doctors and nurses to occupy as they bustled in and out of the room.

"We're exceptionally crowded right now," a nurse smiled as I looked in vain for a place to sit. "Otherwise there would only be two beds, and there would be more room." She smiled again, something I was to learn was a trademark of those wonderful people. "But if you'll give me a few minutes, I'll see if I can find you a chair."

I thanked her and leaned over the side of Charity's crib, trying not to look at the other infants and thus seem nosey or intrusive.

"What's wrong with your baby?" a very young woman asked from right behind me. And that was when I began to become aware that most of the parents of PCMC patients were extremely young—kids in their twenties or maybe early thirties who seemed way too young to be facing such problems as their children were experiencing. Kathy and I were definitely old people in that hospital.

"Shunt surgery," Kathy responded. "To drain the excess fluid from her head."

"Oh," the woman responded as she rose and moved beside me to gaze tenderly at our daughter. "Poor little thing. She looks so tiny and alone. How did it go?"

"We hope just fine," Kathy replied. "We haven't heard otherwise."

The woman nodded. "That's good. Did Dr. Walker do it?"

We nodded.

"Good. He's the best! Another of his patients, a sweet little boy down the hall, is in for his fiftieth shunt revision. He's such a neat little kid—"

"What's the problem with your little girl?" I asked into the awkward silence that had followed her statement.

"She was born with spina bifida. This is her fourth surgery. I'm Carol, my daughter's name is Alyse, and this," she said, indicating the third mother in the room, "is Mary Ann. Yesterday her daughter Heather had surgery for a blocked colon. She's not quite two weeks old."

"Hi," Mary Ann said timidly.

We responded, and from that moment those three women were fast friends, bonded by their close proximity and the pain of their children. By the next day, we were also friends with the doctors and nurses who filed through the door of Charity's room. Most were extremely personable, and it didn't take us long to realize that we had become part of a big and constantly changing family, all of whom seemed as concerned about our little Charity as we were.

I also watched in awe as Kathy began reaching out to the other mothers, tenderly lifting their burdens and shouldering them with them. Within a day or so, she knew the names of almost every mother—and child—on Four West, and she was fast friends with most of them. In spite of her sorrow over our own child's suffering, she visited with the others, wept with them, hugged and held them, and somehow found time and strength to sit with them when crises came. And yet never for a minute did she neglect or forget our daughter.

I had never really seen this side of my wife, and since I am by nature more shy and introspective than she is, I was overwhelmed. In fact, during that four days I fell in love with her all over again, for entirely new reasons.

Often over the next few days I strolled the halls or sat in the crowded waiting room, giving the doctors and nurses space and trying to divert my mind from Charity's pain. Always there were parents or grand-parents in the waiting room, visiting, sleeping, or just staring off into space, too numb from their experience to do anything else. And there were children every-where, for PCMC was a place for children, and for everyone there, children were the focus.

"Kath," I muttered the next day as we walked down the hall toward the elevator, "I can hardly bear to look at these children. It . . . it hurts too much."

Kathy squeezed my hand. "I know, hon. You've never been able to handle seeing people hurting."

"Who could? Especially here, where the ones doing the hurting are innocent little people who don't even understand what's happening to them. I don't care if my kids do tease me about crying too easily. When I'm here, it's all I can do to keep myself from bawling all day long!"

And it was difficult. But who could control their feelings of sympathy and sorrow when all about us were the maimed and tormented little bodies of children? There were children with cancer who had lost all their hair and strength to radiation and chemotherapy; there were accident victims who had lost limbs, eyesight, and so forth; there were victims of abuse who had suffered horrid injustices; there were children like little Charity who had struggled with problems from birth; and there were children who were ravaged by various terrible diseases. I could hardly bear to look at them, let alone begin to comprehend their pain.

Yet unfailingly the personnel at PCMC approached their tragic tasks with smiles and joyful attitudes, doing everything in their power to ease the pain and lift the burdens of the children. To that end the wallpaper and even the little gowns and pajamas were bright and animated. Some hospital personnel wore funny hats and teased the children into rare smiles and laughter. The nurses were unendingly cheerful. Ronald McDonald the clown was a regular visitor who always brought forth wide-eyed stares and giggles. And volunteer grandmas and grandpas came and sat for hours with children whose parents, for one reason or another, could not be there. In spite of the pain and suffering, it was truly a place of love and giving, and each night as Kathy and I lay exhausted but sleepless, discussing the day's events, our conversation would always return to the magic of PCMC that we were feeling.

13

A Personality Becomes Evident

"CAN YOU believe it, Blaine? Look at all these darling little outfits. I think every woman in the neighborhood came to the shower."

Like Kathy, I was amazed by the outpouring of love and concern shown us by our friends and neighbors once Charity was home from the hospital. Knowing we had grown past the "new baby" stage of life, these dear people had responded to the news of our adopting a little girl by setting us up with baby clothing, a stroller, and all sorts of baby things that are only thought of once they're needed.

More, one after another these women had held our daughter and exclaimed at the powerful spirit of love and joy she seemed to radiate.

"I find it so amazing the way she affects people," Kathy stated that night. "It's just like in my dream—person after person stopping me to see and hold Charity and feel her spirit."

"Why not, Kath? *We're* that way." And we were, too. None of the kids seemed able to get enough of holding her, cuddling her, and playing and laughing with her. And I was the worst of the lot. I simply couldn't stop nuzzling and loving her, and I thrived on being in her presence.

What was most amazing to me, though, was her personality. She loved to be held and cuddled, she fussed if she didn't get her bottle on time, she enjoyed taking baths, and more and more her radiant smile was becoming a sought-after reward by all of us. To that end the kids danced with her to loud music, made funny little noises in her ear, tickled her and bounced her on their knees, bundled her up and took her for walks in the stroller, and showed her off at every opportunity. And Kathy and I were constantly singing to her—Kathy sweet lullabies and hymns, and me strange little tunes that I made up on the spot, either telling her how I felt about her or what was going on with the other members of the family. I took a lot of heat from the kids over those songs, but at least Charity seemed to enjoy them, and that is what counted most.

Of course, that meant she was hearing us, one of the senses we had expected her not to have. But not only could she hear, she could hear well! No matter how quiet we tried to be, she could always tell when one of us was near. And she visibly reacted to external sounds. For instance, she loved music (the real kind rather than my singing), but only certain kinds. She tolerated Neil Diamond and his music only if the kids were dancing with her to it. Otherwise, no thank you. She hated all other types of rock and roll and would become ill if she heard very much of it. She did not like country western (my own favorite at the time), and most classical music was stressful to her. On the other hand, she enjoyed children's songs—especially if children were singing them—certain numbers from Walt Disney, and all hymns. And of the hymns, the only ones she would ever coo along with were hymns written specifically about the Savior.

Over and over we watched these reactions of hers, which never varied, and the only conclusion we could reach was that she had brought her musical tastes intact from the realms above. After that, we all began thinking a little more about the kinds of music *we* enjoyed.

It was wonderful having Charity feeling better after her surgery. We thought that was all we could have asked for—at least that's what we thought until suddenly she got her days and nights mixed up.

"Maybe if I was younger," I grumbled at about 2:30 on Thanksgiving morning, "I wouldn't need so much sleep."

Kathy yawned. "Your trouble, honey, is that you got used to the soft life."

"Maybe, but those bags under your eyes aren't just makeup, you know."

"I . . . know." Kathy yawned again. "Maybe if we could sleep when she does—"

"Su . . . re." Kathy had me yawning, too. Or at least something did. And Charity was lying there smiling,

64

absolutely unaffected by the indecent hour. "Isn't there something you can give her?" I asked bluntly. "There are some big football games tomorrow, and I don't want to sleep through them."

"Blaine!"

"Well, we've got to do something! We really do need our sleep."

"You could always give her a blessing. She seems to understand them."

"Kath—"

"All right, O ye of little faith."

Although at first I was dubious, desperation forced me to agree. In my prayer I simply explained to Charity that we were getting older and it would be very helpful if she would sleep at night and remain awake with us during the day. That was all, and it didn't seem to do any good. After the blessing she didn't get sleepy until long after daylight.

However, the next night she slept all night, and except for when she was ill or in pain, she never again got her days and nights mixed up. In fact, the change was so dramatic that we began joking about the fact that we had discovered the sleep all-night-through-blessings technique just six babies too late. What we never joked about, however, was our little daughter's amazing obedience.

14

We Hear from the Birth Family

Though I have only briefly mentioned them, our thoughts went often to Charity's birth family. At the time, we did not know these people, yet in quiet moments Kathy and I often discussed them, wondering what they were like and if they were being comforted by the prayers of gratitude we so frequently offered up in their behalf. How thankful we were that the mother had chosen life for her unborn child. Not only would an abortion have denied Charity the right to experience a little mortality, but it would have denied all of us the divinely orchestrated privilege of loving her and getting to know her incredible spirit. Yet it would be terrifically hard, we felt, for a family to keep their baby daughter and granddaughter and then to give her up. And to be the beneficiary of their loss seemed especially difficult to us.

Occasionally Sharon would come and take Charity to them for a few hours, and we were made comfortable with this by thinking of how we would feel if the reverse were occurring. Then one day Sharon appeared at our door with letters to us from the birth parents and grandparents. They were such sweet letters of support for us, but it was easy to see the pain and sorrow these people felt in their loss.

Charity's birth mother wrote:

> I would just like to tell you how thankful I am for the love you give to our precious little girl. I hope she has given you as much happiness as she has given me. The day she was born was the happiest day of my life. I'm so thankful that I still have the opportunity to see her grow and change. I hope that it hasn't imposed on you in any way. I don't know you, but I have a feeling in my heart that you are kind, loving people who care for our precious little angel baby. Thank you for everything you've done. I'll never forget her and all the joy she's given to me. I'll love her throughout eternity. <u>Love and thanks forever</u>.

It was no wonder, we thought as we read these letters, that Charity was such a special soul.

A Second Surgery

"BLAINE, she's getting head pressure again. I know she is."

I shook my head more in dismay than disagreement. It was snowing outside, there was already six inches on the ground, and the last thing I wanted to do was set out for the hospital in a snowstorm. Besides, it was just a couple of days until Christmas, we had a major celebration planned, and I didn't want to go through the hassle of unplanning it. But those weren't the real problems, and I knew it.

"Look at her soft spot," Kathy continued defensively. "See how it's bulging? That isn't normal, and you know it."

"I wasn't disagreeing with you, Kath. I . . . I just don't want poor little Charity to go through this again. I mean, that shunt is supposed to work for years, most likely for the rest of her life. If it isn't working, it will mean another surgery, and I don't know if any of us can take that again!"

The trouble was that Charity was really starting to struggle, and I couldn't bear that, either. So that afternoon I called Dr. Walker.

"Well, Kath," I said after the call, "he says the shunt might be blocked. That's what keeps happening to that little boy who was operated on when we were there last time."

"So what do we do?"

"Keep her comfortable as much as we can. If there are still problems, Dr. Walker wants to see us right after the holidays."

And there were problems! Twice in the week between Christmas and New Year's, Charity reached such levels of stress that she briefly stopped breathing. She whimpered and cried all the time, her little body was rigid and trembling, and she could hardly bear being touched. Unfortunately, neither could she bear being left alone.

"That is exhaustive for all of us," I wrote to our two older children, Tami and Steve, who were on extended stays in Europe. "But thank goodness Nate, Travis, Dan, and Michelle all love her and are willing to take turns holding her for hours on end. Danny especially has developed the ability to keep her calm and happy, but that may be because he is strong and can hold her upright for longer periods—a position she seems to enjoy.

"We are also noting that Charity can no longer bear the stress of leaving our home. All fall we have enjoyed taking her to church, and she has seemed to enjoy it with us—even occasionally singing. Once she even got on the right note but didn't cut it off when the chorister did. All of us snickered but Michelle, who was embarrassed almost to tears. Anyway, the past few weeks she has not been able to endure more than a few moments in church before she grows all rigid and trembling—the only reason I can think of is that she can't tolerate the noise."

On January 4, 1989, after the doctor had determined that Charity's shunt was completely blocked, a new shunt was surgically implanted—this time on the opposite side of her body from the first one. And once again we and our tragically ill little girl were delivered over to the caring and compassion of the personnel at PCMC.

Following the surgery, one of the nurses noticed that Charity seemed to be having seizures. Dr. Fan Tait, a neurologist, was called in, and she felt an EEG was in order. The EEG was administered on the 7th, and the next morning at 9 A.M. we were invited to meet with Dr. Tait.

Spreading the EEG out on the table, Dr. Tait pointed out the electrical "spikes" Charity was experiencing. "This little girl's life is in danger," she said in a soft Southern accent, her voice filled with genuine concern. "I believe we need to do something fast." Then she explained that individuals prone to seizures might spike every five minutes or so, which was considered serious. Charity's brainstem, on the other hand, was spiking as often as every second or two, a situation Dr. Tait feared would destroy what limited brain tissue she had. Dr. Tait suggested Phenobarbital to control the spiking, and we concurred with her suggestion.

That afternoon as we sat with our innocent little girl, watching her tiny body twitch and suffer from the pain of the surgery and everything else she seemed forced to endure, I finally broke down. "It isn't fair," I said, burying my face in my hands. "Why should an innocent little baby like her be forced to suffer? Why does God allow it? If she's going to die anyway, why doesn't He just take her and stop all this craziness?"

"I . . . don't know," Kathy responded as her tears fell.

"I mean, how can a God of love allow this? She hasn't sinned; she'll never even be capable of sinning. If she's going to automatically return to God's presence, which I believe with all my heart, then what possible reason can there be for her to suffer like this?"

Instead of answering, for she had no answer, Kathy simply reached over and took my hand. At the very least, if we couldn't understand and if we couldn't comfort our forlorn little daughter, then perhaps we could at least comfort each other.

A Major Miracle

WE BROUGHT Charity home on January 9, 1989, and again we were hopeful that we would not need to see the inside of PCMC again. After all, with both surgeries we had spent a total of nine days there, and we thought that surely Charity would now begin acting like the medical experts had told us she should act—no health problems except for congestive things that would ultimately lead to death by pneumonia.

Unfortunately, again both we and they were wrong. Over the next few days Charity seemed to grow more and more ill. We didn't know what was wrong, the doctors didn't know what was wrong, and if Charity knew, she couldn't tell us. All she could do was suffer, and all the rest of us could do was suffer with her.

And then one night—Friday the 13th of January it happened to be—a miracle happened. All day

Charity had grown more and more ill. She was rigid and screaming, and we could do nothing that brought her any comfort. Twice Travis and I blessed her to be at peace, and after the second blessing, when absolutely nothing changed, Travis picked up some object and threw it against the wall.

"What's wrong with God?" he raged in absolute frustration as tears of love and sympathy streamed down his cheeks. "Doesn't He see how much she's suffering? She hasn't done anything wrong! So why doesn't He stop this?"

Weeping with him, for Charity was truly suffering, neither Kathy nor I could offer an answer. We didn't understand it ourselves, so how could we explain it to our son?

"I . . . I'm sorry," Travis said a few moments later. "I know God doesn't cause this stuff. I just wish she didn't have to hurt so much."

"So do we," Kathy declared as she embraced him. "So do we!"

Throughout the day, as Charity continued to scream and tremble with pain, we prayed, singly and together, for some sort of relief. We even pleaded that, if it were possible, she would be allowed to pass away and depart this vale of tears.

Calls to our pediatrician and PCMC brought no ideas on what might be wrong or what we could do, and even a visit to the local emergency room for tests failed to turn up a solution.

Finally, sometime after midnight, as she exhaustedly rocked Charity back and forth, Kathy suddenly stopped. "I think I know what to do," she whispered. "Pour some warm water in the tub."

"Kath, it's nearly one in the morning. It isn't exactly the hour for bathing."

"It isn't a bath, hon. I have a feeling it will help her."

Quickly I poured a couple of inches of warm water into the bottom of the tub. And then, because Kathy's back problems were growing worse through the strain of holding Charity's rigid and arching little body so many hours each day, I took our baby and lay her in the water, her head supported in my hand.

For a few seconds she continued to scream. Then, abruptly, she stopped and looked directly at Kathy and me as though she could see us clearly. For three or four minutes she lay without moving a muscle. And then, to our everlasting surprise, she began kicking both legs at once (she has never been able to do that normally) and splashing her hands and feet in the water.

Then, to our further surprise, she smiled. Only briefly. But she smiled! Then came more splashing, more and bigger smiles, and suddenly, without any warning, she rolled her head back on my arm, her huge smile still there, and began to *giggle*.

We had never seen Charity laugh, had never seen her do anything even remotely close to it. But for the next twenty minutes, as she splashed about in the tub, she giggled again and again. She would splash, roll her head to look at us, and giggle; splash, roll her head to look at us again, and giggle some more. It was the sweetest thing I had ever seen in my life, and as Kathy and I knelt beside her breathing prayers of gratitude, plenty of tears joined the bathwater being joyfully splashed about by our daughter.

After about twenty minutes the giggling and even the smiling ceased, and she was back to kicking with just one leg at a time. We knew that our miracle—of Charity being allowed to play in the tub just like all our other children had done—was over. After we had dressed her, we laid her in her crib, and in just moments she drifted into a sound sleep that lasted until late the next morning. And upon awakening, she seemed to be feeling much better.

Nearly three weeks later, following many additional examinations and tests, I wrote in a letter: "At least part of Charity's problems, it turns out, are because she is allergic to the Phenobarbital. As for her laughter in the tub, no matter what we do that delightful behavior has not repeated itself. She still smiles occasionally and maybe kicks one leg, but there is no laughter or giggling, and the doctors, when we told them of the incident, told us there won't be (never could be, for that matter) because she lacks the brain capacity to express that sort of complex emotion.

"Yet we saw it clearly, which can mean only one thing—with the help of God this tiny child can be granted the capability of performing any activity or function any other child can perform."

Little did I know.

A Letter from Kathy

ONE NIGHT in February, I came upon Kathy weeping quietly on her knees. In response to my query, she told me that she had called a doctor with a question, and he, frustrated because Charity did not seem to keep "normal medical rules," had told her quite sharply that he had no more answers than she did—the implication being not to bother him any more, that we were on our own.

"Heavenly Father is all I have left to turn to," she whispered. "And . . . and you." And then, as we held each other, she broke down and sobbed out her loneliness and grief.

"But I'll tell you what I'm going to do," she suddenly declared, wiping her eyes. "I'm going to learn everything I can about Charity's problem, and I won't stop until I understand her. Then at least somebody will!"

The next day she went to work, studying everything she could get her hands on and grilling every doctor she could talk to with questions so detailed and sometimes so repetitive (she wanted to make certain she was understanding the medical jargon and occasional gobbledegook used by one or two of them to deflect her from seeing their own ignorance) that I grew embarrassed. Still, she kept after them until I was amazed at what she had learned. She also developed wonderful nursing skills as she spent hour after hour caring for Charity. Never had I imagined that someone could so completely devote her life to another.

But as in all things mortal, there was a price. Kathy's back continued to deteriorate. Yet not once, not under any condition, did she allow her own pain to slow her down or diminish Charity's care. She was absolutely tenacious in her twenty-four-hour-a-day service to our little girl, and I will never in this life have words sufficient to express my love and admiration for what she did.

Through the winter and into the spring, Charity struggled with her reaction to Phenobarbital. In March she was hospitalized six days as Dr. Tait ran tests, after which she was switched to Dilantin. She also reacted to that, and after another six days' hospitalization in May, she was switched again, to Clonopin, which she also reacted to. Finally Dr. Tait tried Tranxene, which she tolerated quite well.

Meanwhile, it seemed that our home life was in chaos. The people we were renting from were trying to sell their home and had asked us to show it for them, which we were happy (?) to do. My writing career was behaving more like a broken yo-yo than a rising star. To make economic matters worse, a Medicaid caseworker was threatening to cut off Charity's desperately needed, and officially promised, Medicaid benefits. And there were also the normal problems of having four kids in high school and junior high with all of their activities and challenges, which Kathy especially tried to be a part of. Besides my normal work, I did most of the letter-writing to our two children in Europe, and I spent a lot of time telling them about the new little sister they had never yet seen.

And through it all I watched as two whom I had begun to think of as heaven's daughters—Charity and my dear sweet Kathy—faced each new crisis and challenge with courage but without complaint, with sorrow but without murmuring. And on the good days—the days at home when all the two of them had to deal with were huge patches of eczema, seizures, allergic reactions such as weeks-long bouts of diarrhea and nausea, and all the needs a small baby of necessity has—on these days our home rang with laughter and joy. Somehow Charity brought that out in all of us, no matter what she happened to be experiencing at the moment.

Early that spring Kathy wrote our children:

"Since you have never met Charity, let me describe her for you. She now weighs fifteen pounds, so in spite of what the doctors expected, she is growing normally. Her hair had quite a bit of red in it initially, but now that it has all been shaved off it is coming in a darker brown with no red at all. Yet her eyebrows have a great deal of red in them, so maybe she will have auburn hair. It is still rather thin and short, but on the lower back of her head, left side, is a lovely lock of hair that is probably an inch and a half long— a token apparently left by the surgeons to appease my motherly instincts.

"Charity's skin is the color of pure porcelain, and her eyes are very unusual. When she feels good, her pupils expand until it seems her eyes are completely black. But when her head develops pressure the pupils contract, and then she has the prettiest blue eyes one can imagine. There is a dark outer edge, then lighter blue, then occasionally a very thin line of darker blue before the black of the iris. These gorgeous eyes that I love to gaze into are framed by long, dark, curly eyelashes that any girl would die for. They are very striking.

"Her left nostril is a little misshapen in what is the cutest little button nose. She has what one of my friends calls an 'Arby hat' mouth, very dainty and petite. Her cheeks are very chubby (she reminds me so much of Tami and Michelle as babies that I can't imagine we actually adopted her), and her ears are set close against her head and are so cute. Because of her hydranencephaly, she holds her thumbs in all the time with her fingers usually clenched over them. She stiffens her arms and legs and curls her toes straight down when she is frightened or in pain, and it is very difficult to bend her arms and legs unless she is perfectly relaxed.

"She rarely cries just to hear herself, but she has a good, loud cry when she wants to let it out. But what really breaks my heart is the pathetic little rapid sob she makes when she is in pain. Some of the doctors still don't believe she is capable of pain, but I know very well they are wrong. This child really suffers from pain, and in the moments when she is free of it, her beautiful smile declares her joy to all the world. She also talks occasionally—sweet little baby sounds that I love to hear. But our family's favorite sound is Charity's snort, which is very loud and occurs every time she sighs or takes a deep breath—not infrequently. We have no idea why she does this, but we absolutely love it!

"She is a very patient baby, oftentimes lying in bed for an hour or more after awakening without any complaint. And that, by the way, is the only time we can get her to smile. In the morning, when she is well rested, if we go in and call her name very quietly, she will give the sweetest smile in the whole world. She responds to us at other times by kicking or using her eyes, but our favorite responses are her smiles.

"Of course, her doctors don't believe she is really smiling, but they haven't seen it. One of these days Charity will show them, and they will know.

"Among other things she does that we were told she would never do: she knows her name, recognizes our voices, and responds to each of us differently. It is so interesting to see. Nate is reserved with her, and so she is reserved with him. Travis isn't so much reserved as he is shy around her. He is nevertheless quite protective of her, and he nuzzles her neck with his nose when he thinks he isn't being watched. Charity saves her sweetest smiles for him. Dan and Michelle she loves to play and dance with, and she gets all excited whenever they speak to her. She really loves them, and they know it.

"I have never seen Blaine so in love with a child, and Charity loves him just as much. She especially enjoys all the cute little love songs he makes up for her. They make her absolutely beam! More and more I need his help, so he is now getting up at 4:00 in the morning to do his writing. He says it isn't a problem, but I can tell how tired he is.

"And me? Well, I'm just Mom. I'm the one who has to worry about all the little things like swabbing her mouth to keep it moist, getting her the medications on time, feeding her, keeping her warm (it seems easy for her to get cold), and of course bathing, dressing, and changing her, and doing everything I can think of to make her comfortable. A good share of my day is spent trying to make her more comfortable so she will relax. In fact, I spend hours and hours each day holding and rocking her—and constantly the Holy Spirit whispers 'Cherish these moments.' Charity puts up with all of my fiddling with her body, but sometimes I can tell that she really grows tired of it. Yet I can feel her love for me, too, and it is the most wonderful feeling in the world. Her love makes all of the hard times worthwhile."

18

An Interesting Question

"YOU KNOW, Blaine," Kathy said one day when I came in to spell her with Charity's bottle, "somehow this little girl can think, and I have proof of it."

Reaching down, I lifted Charity and began nuzzling her. "I believe you, hon. But proof?"

"Well, it's proof to me. She knows the single pacifier she likes and always rejects the others. She knows exactly which brand of formula she likes and refuses anything else. She lies flat without complaint, but she protests loudly at both her swing and baby seat. On the other hand, if the children or us swing her or hold her upright in our arms, she doesn't protest at all but seems to enjoy it. To me, these are proofs."

I nodded.

"Charity is anything but a vegetable," Kathy concluded, "and I can't imagine how any thinking person—especially medical people who have been trained to reason—could be deceived into such an idiotic conclusion as so many of them seem to have come to."

As Charity lay in my arms contentedly working her bottle, her fathomless eyes locked on my own, I had to agree. There was definitely an intelligence there, an intelligence that had nothing to do with the human organ called a brain.

When Tami returned from England near the end of February, we learned again how obedient Charity was and how her amazing "mind" operated. Of course, Charity was not used to her voice, and each time she was held by Tami she began to cry. After three days of this, I finally took Charity (again at Kathy's suggestion) and went alone into the living room, where I explained in a blessing who Tami was and how bad she was feeling about Charity's tears.

Charity never again cried in Tami's arms. In fact, the two of them became extremely close, and each learned how to help and love the other. Later Tami wrote: "I'm not sure how to say how I feel about Charity, and how grateful I am that she has been in my life. The words 'I love her' seem so inadequate. Sometimes I feel that trying to thank her is a little like trying to thank the Savior for His love and atonement. Nothing I might ever say could express the depth of my feelings. Every memory of her I treasure. I look forward to the day when we can embrace and talk face to face and I can hear her words as well as feel her incredibly beautiful spirit."

When Steve came home from Norway a couple of months later, having learned my lesson, I immediately gave Charity a blessing of introduction, and without hesitation she welcomed Steve wholeheartedly into her life. "My experiences with Charity and my feelings for her," Steve writes, "have filled me with wonder and profound love. Charity couldn't do much physically, but I have never seen anyone change the lives of so many people for the better. She is a remarkably obedient person."

We were so struck by this ability of Charity's to receive communication and understanding through blessings, that from then on we used blessings to inform her of whatever was happening in our family. For instance, if for any reason Kathy and I were given a brief break together, I first blessed Charity to know that we were leaving only temporarily. She was then peaceful for her tender-hearted caregivers. On the rare occasions when I forgot to do this, however, Charity was broken-hearted by our absence and showed it through her tears.

On 6 April 1989, we all gathered in court, where a judge granted our petition and Charity Afton became our legal daughter. Even the birth certificate filed with the state reflects Kathy and me as her parents. Then, in a sweet religious ceremony on 26 May 1989, Charity was made a spiritual part of our family. Afterward, as we visited, the man who had performed the ceremony made a remark that burned like fire into my thinking, a remark I will not forget as long as I live: "In our church we believe in the ministering of angels," he said as he held Kathy's and my hands from his wheelchair. "It would be interesting to know why you and your family have been selected to minister *to* one."

Well, we didn't know. But with this man's witness, we knew with absolute surety that Charity was indeed an angel from the presence of God—a powerful being of pure sweetness and light who had honored and blessed us with her presence in ways we would never in mortality fully understand.

As Travis, who had only recently traveled to South America, recorded in his journal: "I love Charity tons—she's just an angel. Go ahead. Tell me that sounds strange. But no matter what it sounds like, it is the honest-to-gosh truth. I love partaking of the Spirit that she seems to constantly possess. I love that kid to death, and quite often I find myself missing her."

What mattered that others did not understand or even denied such intangible, spiritual things? What mattered that at times her care seemed hard? What mattered the loss of a little personal freedom, the spending of a few extra dollars, or even hundreds of nights' sleep given up in her service? To have the privilege of dwelling even briefly with one of God's holy angels was worth any price we had to pay.

Just how worth it, we were beginning to learn.

To Discomfort an Angel

A FEW weeks later, during what we were calling one of her "good times," Charity suddenly grew very ill. We couldn't tell what was wrong, the doctors couldn't tell, and even Tylenol didn't bring her any peace. She was absolutely miserable.

Of course, we prayed constantly for help in knowing what to do, but for a week we remained at a loss. Then one Saturday morning while I was pleading for her relief, it suddenly dawned on me that the problem might not be Charity's. Quickly I gathered the family into an emergency session.

"All right, listen up. You all know that Charity is doing badly. Since we can't seem to find a problem with her, I'm thinking that maybe the problem is with one of us."

"What are you talking about, Dad?"

"I'm talking about the fact that she is perfectly pure, without sin. Do you all agree with me?"

Everyone nodded.

"Okay, do you all agree that she will never, no matter how long she lives, have the capacity or desire to commit sin?"

"We all know that, Dad." Dan's mind was racing ahead like always. "What's the point?"

I smiled. "The point is that Charity is truly a heavenly person, the only one I've ever known. In terms of purity, at least, she is just like God, whom the Bible says is perfect. And since God doesn't like sin, what do you suppose might happen if Charity is forced to be around it?"

"She wouldn't like it," Michelle declared.

"How would she let us know she didn't like it? How would she react? Think about this, kids. Suppose one or more of us is doing something wrong. I don't mean the normal little stuff. I mean something pretty major that our conscience is already telling us we shouldn't be doing. With Charity being unable to get away from us because of her circumstances, and being unable to tolerate our sins because of her perfect purity, might her reaction be to get sick?"

Everybody looked at me in amazement, Kathy included.

"Remember," I went on, "I'm not suggesting that we need to be perfect. But I believe we each need to go off alone for a few minutes and search our souls. If I'm right, one of us is having a major problem with sin that we're hiding—only apparently we can't hide it from Charity. If it happens to be you, come tell me quickly, and let's get this taken care of before she suffers any further."

A few moments later one of the kids came quietly into my office, acknowledged an inappropriate book hidden in the home, and asked what should be done. My instructions—and I was playing this completely by ear—were to take the book back to where it came from, apologize to Charity, and then go off alone and apologize to God and seek His forgiveness.

My counsel was strictly followed, and thirty minutes after that Charity was smiling and happy again, with no signs of her former illness about her.

Time and again we observed this phenomenon. Charity reacted almost instantly to wickedness around her—she was not physically able to tolerate it. She even began crying if Kathy and I had a disagreement, which I hadn't thought of as particularly unrighteous until she came along.

In emphasis, Dan wrote: "When I think of Charity, I also think of love. When she first came to our family, we realized quickly the pain that our normal, everyday contentions caused her. Thus she helped us learn to love each other better, and in so doing we were showing the love we had for her. I can say without hesitation that Charity's coming into our lives is the single most important thing that has ever happened to our family."

In every way imaginable, Charity's impact upon all of us was for good. As Michelle put it: "Charity has touched and enriched my life in many ways. She emanates the sweetest spirit. Whenever I found myself struggling, in anything at all, I would always go to Charity's room because I knew an angel resided there. Whatever my problem was, I would pick her up and hold her for a little while, and when I left her room my problems always seemed better. The Holy Spirit felt so near that even just walking into her room made me cry. She has taught me some of life's most important lessons, and I will always love her dearly."

Needless to say, having a little spiritual barometer in our home was a unique experience, occasionally highly discomforting, but always beneficial.

20

My Own Personal Struggles

DESPITE such supernal moments, and laying aside Charity's suffering and Kathy's unending sacrifice in her behalf, my own day-to-day life seemed also to be increasing in difficulty. Forced to move again by the sale of the home we had been renting, it seemed to me that my mind—and my life—were always in chaos. I could never find books and other research materials I felt I needed for my writing (at one point, too tired to think of moving my collection of research books one more time, I had simply given 39 boxes of them away), and I could not seem to focus on the work I was supposed to be doing. In fact, as I sat at my computer one morning in late August, it occurred to me that in three months I had not even completed an entire page in the manuscript I had promised to submit to my publisher the previous spring. For a man who carried the responsibility of recovering financially and of supporting his family's needs, it was hard not to think of myself as a failure. I did a lot of joking to others about being a wanderer and a vagabond upon the earth, but inside myself I knew it was no joking matter.

Worse, while many of our dear family, friends, and neighbors had expressed sweet support for our decision to adopt little Charity, and were helping in whatever ways they could, there were a few, some even within our own extended family, who were very critical (isn't it strange how we can let the opinions of the few affect us more than those of the many). One chose to avoid much association with Charity because she was not of "our bloodline," others continually dropped unsubtle hints regarding our amazing foolishness for adopting her in the first place, and on three separate occasions I was angrily denounced by well-meaning individuals for what I was "forcing" Kathy to endure. The kids picked up on some of this at school, which both confused and hurt them, and one of my brothers, attending a local ballgame one night, listened as some friends of ours seated next to him (but who did not know him) made jokes about our stupidity. It was all he could do to restrain himself from "letting them have it," as he put later.

I did my best to shield Kathy from this nonsense, but nevertheless what she did encounter hurt her deeply, and it had a noticeable effect on me. In fact, there were days when I found myself wondering some of the same things our critics had voiced, and times when no matter how hard I prayed I couldn't seem to find any comfort. Looking back, I can see that I was falling apart as rapidly as were Kathy and Charity. It was just that I was doing it in a different direction.

Thank the Lord we had little Charity in our lives. Her smile could salve even the worst of my wounds, and many were the times when, as I held her and tried to comfort her in her pain, she ended up comforting me even more. I am not able to describe the amazingly soothing effect she had upon my soul. Neither will I ever be able to sufficiently thank God for the great blessing she became to us. What I can do is state that though I didn't understand her pain, I came to know absolutely that her adoption by my family had been no mistake, no foolishness, no stupidity. She was where God wanted her to be, and it became increasingly obvious to me as that summer passed that the blessing was far more ours than it was hers.

Praying for Death

"BLAINE, I'm scared for her. I don't think she can take a lot more."

"I don't either," I said as I held Kathy's hand. "I couldn't, I know that!"

It was the end of August, and now we were back at PCMC, sitting in the waiting room as Dr. Linda Book ran tests concerning reflux problems Charity had apparently developed. It was amazing how many different kinds of problems our little angel had, especially since none of them had anything to do with respiration. In fact, not only had she never come down with any of the normal childhood illnesses, but she had never even had a cold. Once again she was not doing what the medical profession had expected.

However, she had been terribly ill during this hospitalization, so sick and in so much pain that she had lost her ability to suck. For her to obtain nourishment, an NG tube had been inserted through her nostril and into her stomach, a tube that had to be replaced weekly, and from then on she took all her nourishment as well as medications through that tube.

During her hospitalization, Charity spent her first birthday in PCMC, and I was overwhelmed with the way the hospital personnel went out of their way to ensure that not only she, but Kathy and me as well, had a special day. All day long, nurses walked in singing happy birthday songs. Charity was given a beautiful little hand-sewn blanket that had been donated by someone for that very purpose. Balloons and a tiny cake with a single candle were brought in. Even Ronald McDonald came and posed with Charity for our camera. In spite of Charity's struggles, it truly was an enjoyable day—made so, I know, by the extra caring of our PCMC friends.

Many of our family also made the trek to the hospital in order to celebrate with Charity, and it was easy for me to see that this challenged little angel had worked her way as deeply into their hearts as she had mine. One day Nate, twenty-two years old now, came in and stood beside her bed while silent tears streamed down his face. After he was gone, the mother of the other child in the room took Kathy's hand. "I don't think I've ever seen anything so beautiful," she said. "For a boy that age to have the maturity to weep over his little sister is remarkable. I can tell your family really loves her." And she was right. We did.

"You know," Nate said as we walked down the hall together, "I thought you and Mom were crazy for adopting Charity. Since you did, I figured why go to all the trouble and endure the pain that would surely come about through emotional attachment. But she won't let me get away with it. Part of her mission here, I believe, is to teach love to all who come in contact with her, even on the most casual level. And that includes me. She is her name in its purest form, and I can feel her love, Dad. I . . . hope it isn't too late for me to love her back."

I assured him that it wasn't. But to tell the truth, there were one or two people who simply didn't feel her spirit. For instance, a young doctor approached Kathy one difficult night and offhandedly asked if she were ready to pull the plug and let Charity go, for she was dying anyway and wouldn't live more than another few days. Surprised, for none of the other doctors had said such a thing, Kathy told him she couldn't make that decision without me, and that we wouldn't make it anyway unless we knew it was right. The young man shrugged and departed, Kathy was left reeling, and nothing more was said about it.

In September Charity was hospitalized for six days for more tests, which were inconclusive. By the latter part of October, however, it was becoming evident that the shunt was not functioning properly, though no one could be sure why. On November 3 she received a CT scan, and that and other tests, including a serial computerized tomogram, showed evidence that the shunt was overdraining rather than the reverse.

"When you draw too much cerebrospinal fluid from Charity's cranial cavity," Dr. Walker explained, "it creates a situation much like a dry socket where a tooth has been extracted. And like a dry socket, the pain of too much fluid loss in the head is incredible. In other words, Charity is experiencing something like continuous massive migraine headaches."

"Can anything be done?" I asked.

"Well, we can try adjusting the shunt. If that doesn't work, then we'll replace it with a shunt with a higher pressure valve."

In sorrow Kathy and I gazed down at our little daughter, who had finally grown her hair back out. Now, I thought, she was going to have it shaved off once again.

"With pain like that," Kathy said as she focused on the most important thing, "it's no wonder she's been so miserable and uncomfortable. She whimpers and quakes and trembles constantly. Can we do this soon, doctor?"

"Of course. We'll adjust the shunt right away, and then we'll give her a couple of weeks to see how she's getting along."

And so with heavy hearts Kathy and I prepared ourselves to endure another shunt surgery.

Meanwhile, life continued its frantic pace as we went through the process of marrying Steve to his high school sweetheart. Tami had also become engaged to be married, a situation we were all feeling some discomfort over (ultimately it didn't work out), so it was a terribly busy time for us.

To help Charity's overdrainage, we kept her head lowered, and Dr. Walker performed the shunt adjustment in the middle of November. When that was not successful, Charity was hospitalized again, and on December 5 her shunt was removed and another with a higher pressure valve was inserted on the other side.

Taking our suffering little angel home on the 7th of December, we set about trying to get Christmas organized and a little shopping done. But Charity was not doing well at all, and with each passing day, it became more evident that her condition was deteriorating. Less time was spent sleeping—for us as well as for her—and her poor little body was constantly racked with pain.

On the 19th, with Christmas still so far from being ready in our home that it was unbelievable, we were forced to admit our little daughter to PCMC again. There Dr. Walker determined that her newest shunt had malfunctioned, and upon his recommendation we prepared ourselves and our children at home for another ordeal of surgery. To Kathy and me this meant the sorrow of watching one child suffer while older ones at home were neglected. To the children at home, it meant not only that we would be gone sometimes day and night until whenever Charity was ready to be discharged, but also that they might never again see their beloved little sister. It was truly a difficult time for us all.

The removal of the shunt from Charity's right side, as well as the placement of a new shunt on her left side, took place on the 22nd of December. But Charity had been so beaten up by all that had transpired already in her short little life that she did not quickly bounce back. She simply lay in her crib that day and the next, whimpering but not crying, and tearing our hearts out with her almost silent suffering.

"Just look at her," I whispered to Kathy as she was wheeled past us and out the door for another CT scan on the 23rd of December. "How does the poor little thing keep going? And why? Why doesn't she just give up and die."

"Have you prayed for that?" Kathy asked.

"That she can die? Every day, sometimes dozens of times. I love being around her, Kath, but not at this price. I can't stand it! With all my heart I wish she would be taken so she can finally know peace."

"I've prayed for the same thing." Kathy rubbed her tired, red-rimmed eyes. "But I keep wondering. What if Heavenly Father doesn't want her to die?"

I sighed and leaned back in the chair. "I think of that too. I guess you could say I pray out of both sides of my mouth, because even when I'm asking for her to go I'm also asking that, if the Lord wills it, she will be made well so she can stay. To tell you the truth, Kath, I don't know what God wants for her."

"I . . . don't, either," Kathy responded as she wiped some tears that were suddenly escaping. "So lately I've just been praying that you and I can have the strength to endure whatever the Lord has planned."

"I think we're going to need it," I muttered.

"Do *you* think she's going to die?" Kathy pressed. "Soon, I mean?"

Well, I didn't know. But for some reason I didn't think so. At sixteen months of age, Charity wasn't a very big person. Yet despite all the horrors she had been forced to endure, she continued clinging to life with a tenacity that amazed me.

"Not yet," I finally responded. "I don't think she's ready to go."

"Then we'd better pray for her endurance too," Kathy responded as she took my hand. "The way it looks, she must surely know something we don't know, some reason why she feels she must stay."

"But why? Why would God require such a thing of her? I'm telling you, Kath, I don't understand!"

And I didn't, either. It simply made no sense to me that an innocent little child would be required to suffer so deeply, so continually. Neither did I understand why she had been born without a brain in the first place. It wasn't what had caused the intrauterine stroke that was bothering me as much as it was, Why her? Why this perfect little girl?

I didn't know, but it surely didn't seem fair. If people could just see what I had seen over the past sixteen months, I thought. If they could only feel what I had felt as I had watched an innocent child whom I loved suffer and struggle through practically every day of her mortal life! If they could weep as I had wept while watching other little boys and girls toddling into their proud parents' arms or chasing a butterfly or petting a frisky puppy or uttering their first words and then forming them into sentences—if they could see those things and then know that their own little child would never experience such joys, such accomplishments—if they could know that they would never speak with their little girl or communicate verbally, then perhaps they would understand why I was having such a struggle.

Perhaps.

A Startling Discovery

AT SOMETIME around two o'clock the morning of December 24, as Charity was sleeping fitfully, one of the young staff doctors came in to check on her. We visited, and in the course of the conversation I began plying him with the questions that more and more were plaguing my mind.

"I have no idea what happened to cause your daughter's problems," he finally declared, assuming that I was asking only about physical things. "But let's go down to the library, and I'll show you something you might find interesting."

I followed him down the stairs to the PCMC library, which he unlocked and ushered me into. I had not even known such a room existed, but he explained that it was used mainly by the doctors and nurses in the course of their work.

"Hydranencephaly," he said as he opened a large medical text and began thumbing through it, "is a severe manifestation of a disease called fetal alcohol syndrome."

"What?" I was stunned. "You mean Charity's stroke was caused by alcohol?"

The man smiled and held up his hand as if to stop me. "I didn't say that. In fact, it isn't possible to know what caused your daughter's stroke and subsequent hydranencephaly. What I am saying, and you can read about it when I leave, is that diminished brain capacity of one degree or another is the second most common manifestation of the disease called fetal alcohol syndrome."

"So alcohol abuse by the mother—"

Again he stopped me. "Not necessarily by the mother, and not necessarily alcohol abuse, either one. Extensive testing has shown that consumption of alcohol, or the use of drugs, either one, by either parent, can cause fetal alcohol syndrome. And sometimes as little as one or two drinks or a single instance of drug abuse is enough to do the damage.

"Of course, the risk is greater if the mother uses these substances. And the more she uses them, the greater is the chance of damage to her fetus."

"And this may be what happened to Charity?"

The man shook his head. "Again, I'm not saying that. Even if I knew that the history of one or both of your daughter's birth parents revealed substance abuse, I wouldn't say it. I couldn't! Tests would have been needed, tests that were run at the time; interviews conducted and evaluations made. As far as I know, none of that was done.

"Remember, your daughter's intrauterine stroke occurred early in the first trimester of her life. There is every possibility that the birth mother did not even know she was pregnant at the time. Most likely nothing more sinister happened than that she took a painkiller for a bad headache, or perhaps she had a cold and took antihistamines or an alcohol-based cold remedy. That's why pregnant women are warned not to take medications from the moment they even think they might be expecting. Such drugs, or many other things that were out of the control of the birth parents, could have caused your daughter's hydranencephaly.

"So remember, I am *not* giving you information about your daughter. What I am giving you, rather, is the knowledge that tens of thousands of babies born with fetal alcohol syndrome are required to suffer in ways similar to your daughter—most because one or both of their parents were thoughtless or selfish.

"Here. Read this article if you like. When you are finished, turn out the lights and close the door tightly. Perhaps I'll see you tomorrow."

With that, the doctor was gone, and I sat down to read the article he had handed me. A lot of what I read I don't remember, and quite a bit I didn't understand. But on some note paper kept in the library I wrote:

A baby who has fetal alcohol syndrome will exhibit some or all of the following symptoms:

- Lower than average birth weight
- Small or nonexistent brain
- Lower than average intelligence
- Facial abnormalities, including a cleft lip and cleft palate, small eyes, and a small jaw
  - Heart defects
  - Abnormal arm and leg development
  - Poor sucking reflex
  - Irritability
  - Short stature
  - Difficulty sleeping

About a fifth of babies with fetal alcohol syndrome die during the first few weeks after birth. Many of those who survive are physically and mentally disabled.

All right, I thought as I made my way back up to spend the rest of the night with my little Charity that Christmas Eve morning, maybe that was her problem and maybe it wasn't. But meanwhile, what about her? What about what was happening now? Where was the justice in her suffering? Where was the purpose? Why didn't God intervene? Why couldn't He make at least one thing right in her life? Why—

A Christmas Outpouring

I WAS watching but not seeing the lonely, tattered angel on top of the Christmas tree when a group of carolers moved through the waiting room. Blinking to clear my mind, I glanced at the clock and discovered, to my surprise, that I had been sitting there more than an hour. With a heavy sigh, I rose to my feet and headed back to Charity's room. Probably, I thought, Kathy would need a break.

"The First Noel" and "Silent Night" were the songs the carolers were singing as I made my way past them, songs celebrating the birth of Christ. But in my loneliness and sorrow, the words bounced off me, making no impression.

"Honey," my wife suggested as I came through the door, "why don't we both go downstairs to attend church?"

"I know we need a break, Kath. But what about little Charity? One of us should stay here with her."

"I'll take care of Charity," a young nurse said brightly as she came into the room and into our conversation. "As a Christmas present, of course. You two go ahead and go. You both look like you could use a break."

"What were you doing?" I grumbled teasingly. "Eavesdropping?"

She laughed, not sounding tired even though she had been on a constant run from crisis to crisis since seven that morning. Quickly she shut off a piercing alarm and began readjusting the lead wires to our baby's chest. "Nurses have 20/20 hearing," she replied as she worked. "That's part of our training. Besides, I'd love to spend more time with your darling little girl. She just radiates Christmas cheer! Now hurry or you'll be late."

I smiled weakly and thanked her. Then together Kathy and I gave a longing look at our tiny daughter and departed for the bottom floor of the hospital, where church services were being held.

"Isn't it interesting," Kathy said as we walked, "how Charity affects people? Even those who hardly know us go out of their way to come in and say hello to her."

Silently I nodded.

"Here Charity is almost totally limited in her ability to interact," she continued, "and still she radiates a peace and love that is perhaps the most contagious thing in the hospital."

Stepping to the side of the hall, we smiled as my group of carolers moved past, their words ringing into the rooms of the suffering children: *"Hark, the herald angels sing, glory to the newborn King—"*

"I'm also touched that so many people are willing to give so much for others. Like those carolers. They don't have to be here, and this is about as unresponsive an audience as they could find. Yet here they are, all dressed up and singing like the angels they represent. It's really touching, don't you think?"

"It's Christmas, Kath. People do those things on Christmas."

"We aren't."

I sighed, trying not to feel defensive. "That's because of our circumstances with Charity, and you know it. Besides, it's hard to go around singing and laughing when your little daughter is hanging somewhere between life and death with no real hope for tomorrow."

"I admit it's painful to see her suffering," Kathy continued as we walked along, skirting a Christmas fairy, a priest and two nuns, and several scurrying nurses. "But I'll say one thing: I don't think we could ever find more caring people than those who serve here."

"Or braver parents," I added as we stepped aside for a mother who was maneuvering her wheelchair-bound child and her child's I.V. stand toward us. "I don't know how they handle it. I don't think I could have handled it when I was their age. In fact, I'm not sure I'm handling it now!"

Kathy looked at me but said nothing, the woman with the child and the I.V. smiled and wished us

Merry Christmas, and moments later we entered the gaily decorated elevator. But I wasn't thinking of Christmas decorations as we descended. Instead, I was pondering the young mother's seasonal wishes and bright countenance, and I was still marveling at her upbeat spirit as we entered the basement auditorium where the services were to be held.

We had never attended the ecumenical Sunday service at the Medical Center before, and I watched with interest as people associated with the hospital took care of the program. One of the staff took charge, and the mother of a patient led the singing—all Christmas hymns that day. A sister of another patient played hymns on the piano, a young patient prayed, and two fathers of very ill babies and a young man wearing an awkward-looking brace who turned out to be a long-term patient made some appropriate remarks.

I watched all these people giving service, thought of the pain each of them was covering up but still feeling—pain I had never imagined existed until we had been granted our own challenged daughter—and suddenly I realized that I was weeping.

I'm sure I mentioned earlier that I have a tendency to weep at the drop of a hat, but somehow I sensed that this was different—very different. For one thing, I could not stop. I could not even slow down. For another, my chest felt like it was on fire, and I was trembling visibly, something else I could not stop.

"Are you all right?" Kathy whispered anxiously as she reached and took my hand.

I nodded, fumbling for my handkerchief. "I . . . I feel so strange, so on fire—"

"Are you sick?"

"No! Not at all. In fact, it's the most wonderful feeling I have ever had, like I'm being consumed by the Spirit—"

Scant moments later my wife wiped at her own eyes and squeezed my hand. "I . . . feel it too," she whispered. "The only other time I ever felt like this was that day—"

She stopped speaking, for she had no need of going further. I too was remembering the experience, perhaps the most sacred moment of our marriage, a moment that had come after a lengthy period of great difficulty and much fasting and prayer, a brief hour when both of us had felt an incredible outpouring of the Holy Ghost. In fact, in the dozens of times we had discussed it since, we had both concluded that being in the actual presence of Jesus Christ would surely feel something like how we had felt that day.

Now that same overwhelming feeling was back again, so powerful that even now I cannot describe it. But there was a difference between this and what had happened before, I felt—a major one. Before, the experience had been a result, I had always believed, of our faith and efforts at repentance. But today that was not so. I had the feeling that we were simply bystanders, witnesses to a spiritual phenomena that had more to do with the children in the hospital than it did with us. I didn't understand this spiritual event, of course, but over the years

I have come to accept a great deal of what I don't understand—accept, enjoy, and move onward. And that's what I decided to do with this one.

After the service, we returned to the fourth floor, discussing our experience as we slowly climbed the stairs. The intense spiritual feeling had lasted at least thirty minutes, and then, just as suddenly as it had come, it had gone again. We marveled at that, marveled that we should have been allowed to share it, and, alone once again with our suffering little Charity, we gave silent thanks that the Lord had allowed the power of His Spirit to bring us comfort that day.

The Dishwasher

LATER I sat alone in the cafeteria. Kathy had eaten first and I had followed, eating separately so that one of us could remain with Charity. As I took my first bite, I noticed a young man watching me. He was an employee, a dishwasher I thought, and I knew that he was mentally challenged.

"Oh, no," I thought as I saw his sober gaze resting on me. "I hope he doesn't want to sit with me. I don't feel like making conversation with someone like him—not today. There is so much that I want to think about, to ponder."

I watched furtively and was relieved when he finally sat at the next table. Slowly I continued to eat, but I could tell that he wasn't eating. In fact, even without looking I knew that he was simply waiting, watching me. He hadn't even touched his food.

"Come on," I grumbled at him in my mind, "just eat your dinner. Can't you tell I want to be left alone?"

Still the young man said nothing; he just watched me. So I took another bite, and as I did so, from out in the hall came the sounds of another group of Christmas carolers—*I heard the bells on Christmas day Their old familiar carols play, And wild and sweet the words repeat Of peace on earth, good will to men.*

As I listened to the song, from out of nowhere something inside me spoke—a voice I recognized immediately as my own occasionally hyperactive conscience.

"What's the matter with you?" I was asked rather abruptly. "Don't you believe in Christmas?"

"Sure I do," I stated in surprise.

"Then why don't you act like it?" the inner voice questioned. "You enjoyed a marvelous spiritual experience this morning wherein the Lord spoke great peace to your soul. Where is your *good will to men* that you cannot reach out and speak peace to the soul of another?"

"I . . . uh—"

"Did you think that the Spirit came only to bless and comfort you?" the voice persisted. "Or the physically ill? Did you think that, outside of the little children who are patients here, you and your wife were the only ones who felt it? You know very well that Jesus suffered in order that He might bring peace and comfort to all His children, no matter what their age or why they are suffering. Like the little angel on the tree upstairs, they are also tattered. But Christ loves them more for that, not less, and they remain His angels still."

"I . . . I hadn't thought of it quite like that," I stammered to myself as I saw in my mind the angel on the

Christmas tree upstairs, the angel who had been so abused and battered by others, the angel *I* had been so critical of.

Suddenly my mind was filled with images of the children in the hospital, the ones I had seen that very morning. In one room a child who was battling leukemia had been playing a game with his mother. He was hairless, but he was also smiling, so at least the nausea from his chemotherapy was gone. Two rooms I had passed were isolation rooms where the children were suffering with RSV, Respiratory Syncytial Virus, which led to bronchiolitis. Highly infectious, these isolated children seemed to be in a great deal of pain. In another room lay a tiny girl who had been born with Ventricular Septal Defect, a hole between the lower chambers of her heart. She had also been born without corneas in her eyes, and there had been much urgency as the staff tried to ready her heart so she could have the strength to undergo cornea transplants. I had also seen children who suffered from gastroenteritis and meningitis and various traumas caused by accidents of one sort or another. In fact, I had been told that one entire unit in the hospital was the multiple trauma unit, where children with multiple organ injuries from accidents, abuse, and so forth were cared for.

Indeed they *were* tattered angels, every single one of them! And every one of them was loved of Christ.

"You need to think of them," I was told. "And you need to repent while you're at it. After all, this *is* Christmas. If God the Father and His Beloved Son could send forth Their Holy Spirit on a Christmas visit to all these children, and if seeing pain in these innocent ones is as distressing to you as you have been claiming, then couldn't you perhaps give a little time and love to one who must suffer much longer than your Charity will ever need to suffer—a little *peace on earth, good will to men?*"

Instantly I was encompassed with great guilt. And slowly I nodded my head.

"Besides, my friend," the voice of my conscience continued, now gentle again, "you have always loved Christmas. Here is a chance to make this one just a little bit better than any you have ever enjoyed."

Feeling terrible, I solemnly apologized to heaven for my arrogance. Then, with the beginnings of a genuine smile, I turned to meet the gaze and welcome the amazing friendship and Christ-like love of one tattered angel—one of the Savior's truly elect on this earth.

The Warm Spirit

"Are you alone?" he asked the instant my gaze met his. His face was gravely serious.

Slowly I nodded.

"Can I eat with you?"

I suppose I still hesitated briefly. But then I nodded again and agreed. Quickly he stood, picked up his tray, and stepped to my table.

"My name's Fred," he told me as he carefully arranged his tray and sat down. "What's your name?"

I told him.

"That's a good name," he said sincerely. "I have a warm spirit. Want to feel it?"

Surprised at his question, I wondered how to respond. After all, I knew that this young man was mentally deficient, at least to some extent. But he was also very polite, and though he had not smiled even once, which seemed a little strange, my inclination was to treat him as I would treat any other adult. But his question—

"You say you have a warm spirit?" I asked.

"Uh-huh. Want to feel it?"

"Sure," I replied, trying not to grin. "Only, how do you feel—"

But before I could finish my question, Fred reached out and, with quite a bit of force, clapped his hand on my head just above my forehead.

"See how warm my hand is?" he asked matter-of-factly. "That's because of my warm spirit."

For a moment I sat in startled silence, almost stunned by the incredible warmth of Fred's hand. It *was* warm, almost hot, but it was definitely not unpleasant. For a moment I wondered how my own hand would feel—

"Do you have a warm spirit?" he asked as he suddenly pulled his hand away, almost as if he were reading my mind.

"I . . . I don't know. I—"

"Here," he said, reaching out and taking my hand in his. "Put it on my head and let me feel."

I let my hand be guided to his head. He held it still for a few seconds, then gently he took it away. "It's a little warm," he declared as he took his first bite of food. "Not as warm as mine, though. Do you know why mine is so warm?"

Dumbly I shook my head.

"Because I love people," he said simply. "Love is what makes my spirit warm."

"How . . . do you know that?" I asked slowly while

I remembered my struggle even to want to visit with him.

"My friend told me. Are you glad it's Christmas?"

"I am," I responded, momentarily wondering who his friend was. "I love Christmas."

"Me too. Does that hurt? It looks like it hurts a lot. I'll bet it does, doesn't it?"

Glancing down, I saw that Fred was pointing at the blackened nail of my left forefinger, smashed when we were moving months before. I was startled that he had noticed it but even more startled at the genuine concern and even pain that filled his voice.

"No," I quickly told him, "it doesn't hurt. It did once, but no more."

"Oh, that's good," he breathed with relief. "I hate to hurt. I fell once and hurt my head. It was awful. My friend says I have limitations. Do you know what limitations are?"

Once again caught off-guard, I struggled to formulate an answer. "Uh . . . why don't you tell me," I finally suggested.

Fred nodded agreement. "Limitations are when I can't do all the things that other people do," he stated quickly. "I have limitations here in my head. But my friend told me that as long as I have a really warm spirit, my limitations won't matter. Then after I die I won't have limitations any more. Does the bus go past your house?"

"Uh . . . the bus? No, I . . . uh—"

"I have an apartment of my own, and I ride the bus up here to work. When I hurt my head, it was because I fell off the step of the bus. The snow made it slick. Does that hurt?"

Again I looked down to where he was pointing, and this time Fred had spotted a small scab on my other hand, a scab I had not even realized was there. Gently his forefinger was touching it.

"No," I replied as I shook my head in wonder. "I don't even remember hurting it."

"That's good," he said, once again with definite relief in his voice. "It isn't fun to hurt. My friend says that if I can keep my warm spirit, after I die I won't ever hurt again. If a warm spirit is caused by love, why isn't your spirit as warm as mine?"

I don't think I even answered him that time. The question was too direct, too abrupt, and the answer was too painful.

"Here," he said, I believe sensing my discomfort, "let me feel your spirit again. See? It's getting warmer—a little. My friend says that means you are getting more love. Do you have someone in the hospital you are visiting?"

"Yes," I replied as I pulled my hand back to feel it for warmth that I truly hoped was there. "My baby daughter is upstairs. She . . . has limitations, too. In fact, when she was born, God didn't give her all she needed in order to live. Now she is slowly dying."

"Then she has a *really* warm spirit, doesn't she."

"Yes," I said quietly, "I suppose she does."

"Did you know that Jesus has the warmest spirit of all?"

"I . . . hadn't ever thought of it . . . like that."

"He does. My friend told me so."

More and more I was admiring the wise counsel of this unnamed friend, a person I would likely never know. But oh, the wonderful labor he was performing with this young man named Fred; and through Fred, with others.

"You love your friend, don't you," I said.

"I love everybody," Fred replied simply.

I didn't know how to respond to such a sweeping declaration of righteousness, especially when it was made with such absolute sincerity. So I did the only thing I could do—I changed the subject.

"What do you like best about Christmas?"

Fred looked at me as though he was contemplating an answer, though I was soon to learn that such was not the case. Instead, he threw me another curve.

"Did you know that Jesus came to the hospital today?" he abruptly asked.

"Huh? I mean . . . Jesus *what?*"

Fred gazed at me soberly. "Jesus came to the hospital," he repeated matter-of-factly. "For His birthday. It's Christmas, you know. Christmas is for celebrating Jesus' birthday. My friend says I will have a family after I die, that I can have Christmas with. That's because I won't have limitations any more. Why do you think Jesus came to the hospital?"

"Uh . . . I . . . uh . . . Why . . . uh . . . would you think?" I asked, for the first time in the conversation seeing no recourse but to take the offensive.

"Oh," he said, still very serious, "I already told you, but I just wondered if you heard. He came because it's Christmas, and He wanted to help us celebrate His birthday. He came down here in the kitchen to see me, too."

"He did?" I asked, no longer surprised by anything this young man might say. "I . . . uh . . . how do you know that?"

Fred looked at me seriously. "He loves me, you know. He is my friend. That is why my spirit is so warm today. I think when He came to see me and wish me Merry Christmas and Happy Birthday, He gave me some of His warm spirit to help mine be warmer. If the bus ever comes to your house, can I come see you?"

"Why . . . uh . . . certainly," I replied, still trying to comprehend Fred's simple but great faith. "I'd like that."

For a moment or so Fred ate in silence, but I ate nothing. I believe I toyed with my food a little, but my mind was racing too much to eat. Jesus had come to the hospital. Jesus had come to the—

Suddenly I sat straight with realization. *Jesus had come to the hospital!* The incredible outpouring of the Spirit that my wife and I had felt during the church service—might that have been one and the same event?

"Fred, what time did Jesus come?"

"A little while ago," he answered after clearing his mouth of food. "This morning, just before everybody came to eat. This is good gravy."

I nodded in agreement, but my mind was still scrambling, trying to believe that what my wife and I had experienced might have been an actual visit by the Savior of the World. That was a real stretch for my faith, but as I bandied the idea about, I suddenly realized that a passage from the book of John was going through my mind, around and around as if it were on a drum. It declared, ". . . but Jesus hid himself . . . going through the midst of them, and so passed by."

Now, abruptly, I realized that the Holy Ghost had brought that scripture to my mind. Just as abruptly I found myself truly believing that we had been in Christ's presence, for the burning and the trembling and the weeping, the overwhelming emotion of love I had felt, had been so transcendent that I could not imagine it could be caused by any other thing.

But why had He come? I started to ask myself. I say started, because that is as far as I got. Instantly—once again, I am certain, through the inspiration of the Holy Spirit—my mind was filled with the answer. As it came, my tears started flowing all over again, for the answer was as Fred had already told me. What my sweetheart and I had experienced, I now knew, had been a tender visit by the Savior of the world to some of His sweet, pure, innocent ones, little tattered angels who were suffering so much pain on this eve of the day marked on the calendar as His birthday. Surely on this Christmas He had been in the midst of them, yet for the most part He had hidden himself from the rest of us.

"Do . . . you know . . . why I believe Jesus came?" I asked Fred in a broken whisper.

"Why?" he asked soberly.

"If I am right, then I think He came because He understands my little Charity's pain—hers as well as the pain of the rest of His innocent ones who are here, including you—and He weeps with their suffering just as I weep."

Fred said nothing, only watched me.

"That is why only His suffering innocent ones were recipients of His visit."

Fred remained silent.

"How He must long for the world to finally accept Him and to become pure enough to be in His presence all the time. Only then will we all be allowed to feel that joy; only then will all of this pain and suffering finally be done away with—"

"I'm very careful on the steps of the bus," Fred stated suddenly, as though I hadn't even been speaking. "That's because I don't want to hurt my head any more. I'll be careful when I come to see you. Are you through eating?"

I nodded.

"I can't go upstairs where the babies are, but I can walk up and down the hall. Can I walk to the bottom of the stairs with you?"

I nodded again. We picked up our trays, and in silence we handed them through the window to another dishwasher. Then we turned and walked down the hall to the foot of the stairs.

"Would you let me shake your hand?" Fred asked as we paused.

Eagerly I took his hand and was surprised at the firmness of his grip. The firmness and the warmth.

"Can I shake your other hand?"

Somewhat awkwardly I shook his other hand.

"Your spirit is getting warmer," he said, encouraging me along just as I used to encourage my children when they were small. "Can I have a hug?"

Silently I nodded, and so Fred put his arms around me and pulled me close. Then he held me, his cheek pressed tightly against mine. After what seemed a long time, he pulled away and looked at me.

"Your spirit is much warmer than it was. When you hug me, does it make you nervous?"

"Why?" I asked, feeling guilty because it had.

"Some people don't like to hug. They think it is bad. But they don't have very warm spirits. I like you a lot. Can I have another hug?"

We hugged again, shook hands twice more, and still without a smile, Fred told me that he loved me. That was when I decided to ask him.

"Fred, do you ever wish you didn't have . . . limitations? I mean, do you ever think you got handed a raw deal in life? Don't you get tired of things being so hard all the time?"

His countenance very serious, Fred regarded me in silence. In fact, he was quiet so long that I wondered if he had even understood my questions. I was about to ask them again, using different words, when he finally responded.

"When I hurt my head, I told my friend that hurting was very hard. He told me that when things got hard for me, it just meant that Jesus loved me lots."

"But wouldn't Jesus want to help you—to stop your pain?" I asked, forgetting for a moment that I was speaking with a young man who knew Jesus personally.

"Hurting *does* help me," Fred answered with absolute certainty. "It helps me to feel like Jesus felt when He hurt. My friend said that all Jesus' life he had hard things happen to Him, just like me. He told me to remember that Jesus wasn't born in a hospital like this but in a barn. He was wrapped in ragged old clothes, and they made his bed out of a smelly place where animals ate."

Jesus, too, was tattered, I thought with surprise. Jesus Christ was also tattered—

"If Jesus hadn't hurt a whole bunch, more even than me, my friend says he couldn't have been my Savior." Fred paused, looking at me. "But even when he hurt, Jesus was always happy. My friend says I should be happy too—happy I have been blessed to be like Him. That's why I'm happy. I'm always happy!"

"And . . . your limitations?" I pressed. "Don't you wish you didn't have them?"

"If I didn't have limitations," Fred declared slowly, patiently, I believe making sure that I understood, "I wouldn't have such a warm spirit. That would make it much harder for me to be Jesus' friend. I'm happy I'm His friend, because today He came to see me and wish me Merry Christmas and Happy Birthday."

Then, without another word, Fred turned and walked away.

Silently I stood watching him, trying my best to sort out the incredible array of emotions I was experiencing, the deep understanding I had been given. Fred was happy in his limitations, in being a tattered angel, because that helped him be more like Christ. He did not think he had been given a raw deal. He did not—

And suddenly I knew, if I could have spoken with my tiny daughter—if I could have talked with her for just five minutes about her seemingly unfair pain and suffering—she would have told me the same thing! "It was worth it!" she would have said "It was worth every agonizing moment—"

Filled with rejoicing that I now understood God's love for His tattered angels, His reason for allowing them to suffer, I was just turning to hurry up the stairs when the voice of my new friend spun me back around. "Someday when the bus comes to your house," Fred called out from halfway down the hall, "I will come to see you. Then I can feel your little girl's warm spirit, and she can feel my warm spirit. She has limitations like mine, so Jesus loves her a lot, just like He loves me. My friend says that limitations are what make us special to Him. I'll bet Jesus came to wish your little girl Happy Birthday too."

As Fred spoke so matter-of-factly of Christ's visit, I thought once again of my feelings from earlier in the day, my overwhelming sense from the Holy Spirit that I had also been in His presence. And suddenly I understood the most important thing of all about

God's tattered angels, His imperfect and suffering sons and daughters.

"Yes," I replied softly, "He did come to see her. In fact, He came here to wish Merry Christmas and Happy Birthday to everybody—every single one of His tattered angels.

"Thank you, Fred, for helping this one to see."

And then, filled with the beginnings of that hope in Christ which surpasses understanding and makes all things bearable, I turned and flew two steps at a time toward my precious wife and daughter—

The Rest of the Story

SEVEN years have now passed since Charity Afton came into our home, and five and a half years have gone by since that Christmas season and her last surgeries. Following the Savior's visit, she grew rapidly worse until, in February of 1990, spinal meningitis was confirmed. She did not respond to the massive doses of antibiotics but continued to decline until it was felt by the medical people that she had at most four days to live. At that point, upon Dr. Walker's sympathetic recommendation, we made the difficult decision to remove her shunt, discontinue all medications except those for seizures, and take her home to pass away surrounded by our family.

That evening with all the family gathered around, we sang some of Charity's favorite hymns and had family prayer. Then my father and I and a dear friend gave her a final blessing. We told her that we loved her but that we understood it was time for her to go, and we supported her in it. We closed her blessing in the name of the Lord Jesus Christ just as the apostle James instructed, laid her in her bed, and then waited. And waited. And waited—

And we still are—waiting, I mean—though we're no longer certain what we're waiting for. On her own (save for the Savior), Charity slowly recovered. Now, five-and-a-half years later, she remains alive and grows increasingly alert, and so they have been wonderful years, sometimes difficult but always rewarding. Many times she has led us right to the edge of eternity, and though we have taken no heroic medical measures since the meningitis, Charity has always come back on her own, apparently convinced there is more work she must do with us. And we don't mind her staying, even a little.

Contrary to all expectations, she has grown and is the size and weight of a typical seven-year-old. She has even started to lose her baby teeth and grow in her permanent ones, though because she still gets all her nourishment through NG tubes, what she intends doing with those teeth beyond forming dazzling smiles is a mystery to us.

She continues to resist all typical diseases and illnesses, including the common cold. She is absolutely never sick from these things. However, she has many allergies, she has developed severe osteoporosis, her hips have grown out of their sockets, she has occasional but short-lived bouts with increased pressure from cerebrospinal fluid, and neurological damage has caused a pulling of her head to one side and a painful contracting of the muscles and tendons in her arms and hands.

Despite such problems, Charity has a brilliant, unconquerable spirit. When she feels well, she displays an awareness of her environment, both seen and unseen, that runs much deeper than ours. She joys in our company with unfailing smiles and laughter. She even "talks" to us with little sounds that vary according to the circumstances but are always consistent. For instance, she eagerly plays what we call the "O" game—one of us makes a soft "Oooo" sound, and again and again she repeats it after us, smiling widely and stopping only when we do.

Specific kinds of noises, including those from vacuum cleaners, low-flying aircraft, and running water, frighten her, though other noises don't bother her at all. She at least sees light and actively twists her head about seeking it when we turn out all the lights. She is initially uncomfortable around strangers but quickly responds to their outpourings of love. She endures pain courageously but is certainly affected by it. She absolutely cannot tolerate contention or other forms of unrighteousness within our family, and lets us know how she feels in the most convenient way available to her. She—well, I could go on, but there is no need. Obviously she is not brain-dead. In fact, save for the physical limitations brought about by having no brain, she is a perfectly normal human being.

No, that is not entirely true, for Charity is more than that, so very much more. What an honor it has been for me to know her and for this brief time to reside in her sweet and innocent presence.

As I conclude my account, a light skiff of snow has just fallen—the first of the season. Soon we will be celebrating Christmas again, and I am amazed that it will be Charity's eighth. Who would ever have thought it? And though this Christmas will be as wonderful as all of them have been, with our children and grandchildren gathering from every direction to join Kathy, Charity, and me in a joyous celebration of Christ's birth, I will never forget *that* Christmas.

I will never forget the pain and the trauma, the caring and the courage I witnessed at Primary Children's Medical Center. I will never forget the overwhelming spiritual presence my sweetheart and I were blessed for a few moments to feel, a blessing that may never in our mortal lives come again. And most of all, I will never forget how a humble dishwasher and a child with no brain came together during a tiny but incredible slice of eternity to give me a momentary glimpse of what most of us tattered mortals only aspire to, at Christmas or at any other season of the year—an intimate and lasting friendship with our blessed Savior, the Lord Jesus Christ.

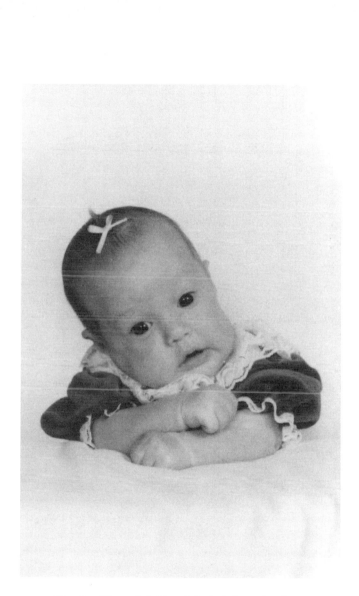

Charity Afton—bright and alert at six weeks of age.
(Photo courtesy Kiddie Kandids)